A Garment Woven
in Victory

Lutheran Comfort in the Resurrection

CAROL GEISLER

Northwestern Publishing House
Milwaukee, Wisconsin

Cover illustration by Susie Weber.

All Scripture quotations, unless otherwise indicated, are taken from the HOLY BIBLE, NEW INTERNATIONAL VERSION®. NIV®. Copyright © 1973, 1978, 1984 by International Bible Society. Used by permission of Zondervan Publishing House. All rights reserved.

The "NIV" and "New International Version" trademarks are registered in the United States Patent and Trademark Office by International Bible Society. Use of either trademark requires the permission of International Bible Society.

Library of Congress Control Number: 2002113511
Northwestern Publishing House
1250 N. 113th St., Milwaukee, WI 53226-3284
© 2003 by Northwestern Publishing House
www.nph.net
Published 2003
Printed in the United States of America
ISBN 0-8100-1513-7

Contents

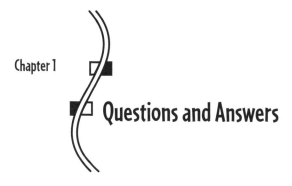

Chapter 1

Questions and Answers

Death is unrelenting and insistent. It is an ongoing process, a very busy thing. In the days before my mother's death, my family experienced the quiet efficiency of the intensive care unit, the compassion of doctors and nurses, Christ-centered pastoral care, and the concern of people we hardly knew sharing with us long hours in the waiting room. My father, my sister, and I were with my mother when she died. By faith I certainly understood that she had fallen asleep in Christ. I knew that at the moment she left us, she entered the presence of her Savior.

Promises of Scripture came to mind. I remembered Jesus' words: "Today you will be with me in paradise" (Luke 23:43), and Saint Paul's desire "to be away from the body and at home with the Lord" (2 Corinthians 5:8). But even with that knowledge, it was hard to ignore the evidence in front of my eyes. I knew my mother was in heaven, but I still saw her there on the hospital bed. The evidence pointed more clearly to death than to life, and faith came into conflict with fact. My struggle was small, perhaps more dilemma than doubt.

In the following weeks, the nagging questions and contradictions didn't really resolve themselves. It happened that during those same weeks I was doing some research for a paper about Martin Luther's teachings on Christ's resurrection. It was Luther, preaching a funeral sermon almost five centuries before, who provided the missing answers and resolved the contradictions. He insisted that, when faced with death, we turn away from the evidence of our senses, from what our eyes see and our ears hear. Instead, we must listen to the Word of God and cling to the promises of the risen Christ. The as yet unseen resurrection life must be more real for us than the visible experience of death. The assurance of faith must outweigh the judgment of human reason.

In his sermons and lectures, Luther used Christ's resurrection as his foundation in addressing critical issues of life and death. He was not afraid to answer questions that—if we're honest enough to admit it—we have all had at some point: What will death be like? What happens to the soul? What will happen on the Last Day? Am I ready to die? Do I have *enough* faith to *die* in faith?

In so many of his writings, Luther revealed his pastor's heart, speaking to people who might soon find themselves at death's door wondering if God really loved them quite as much as they thought. In his discussions of the resurrection, Luther directed the defiance and sarcasm often aimed at Rome at a different target—death.

Luther did not hesitate to speak directly on uncomfortable issues, and he was often more than a little grim in his realistic discussions of death and the grave. He confronted the same issues in his own life, addressing letters of comfort to his parents as they faced what turned out to be terminal illnesses. He expressed outrage at death for taking his young daughter and displayed for us his struggle between human grief and Christian hope. He used ordinary events—farming, planting, giving birth, and traveling—to carry the extraordinary event of the first Easter into our lives.

Luther recognized the conflict between faith and doubt, between God's Word and the evidence of reason. In answer to that conflict, he issued a challenge for us to confront death and life with the defiance and hope found in Christ's empty tomb. Luther understood the resurrection of Jesus Christ to be the chief article of faith, and he wrote of the benefits granted to believers through that Easter event.

Luther found the resurrection in the first messianic promise of Genesis and followed that promise of victory through the pages of the Old Testament. He often stressed the personal nature of Christ's work in the life of the believer. He spoke of Baptism as the event that connects our lives to the life of the risen Christ.

Luther told how faith is nourished through the Word and the sacraments until that day when, with resurrection life and hope, we stand defiant in the face of death. He teaches us to look at the indignity of burial through the framework of Christ's resurrection and to commit our souls into the Savior's care. Luther teaches the certain hope of a life more real than the one now lived. It is a hope woven into our lives from the day we are baptized until its final fulfillment at the resurrection on the Last Day.

The gathered believers who listened to the reformer preach funeral and Easter sermons in the 16th century felt the same fear and sorrow we feel. Like us, they had questions and looked for answers as they stood beside the beds and at the graves of their loved ones. Because of that common experience, Luther's centuries-old teaching is worth hearing today. He found the answer to life and death, to fear and doubt, in an event that was centuries older still. Like Saint Paul, Luther understood the resurrection of Jesus Christ as the death-defying event that becomes part of our lives through Baptism. And along with Saint Paul, Luther saw death not only as an event at the end of a person's life but as a great enemy, the "last enemy to be destroyed" (1 Corinthians 15:26).

Death is an insistent event and an unrelenting enemy, but it is an enemy that has been overcome by the even more insistent event and the unrelenting hope that is the resurrection of Jesus Christ.

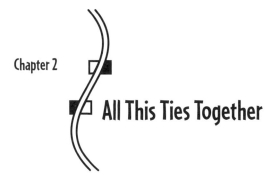

Chapter 2

All This Ties Together

A cartoon character tugs at a loose thread dangling from the sweater of another character. He continues to pull the endless thread, unraveling the entire garment, spinning the wearer like a top and, in the end, leaving the unfortunate creature quite bare.

For Martin Luther, the resurrection of Jesus Christ is like that critical thread, a strand woven throughout Christian life, binding together all articles of faith. If that thread is pulled free, the whole structure of Christian faith unravels, leaving the Christian stripped of all hope and peace.

The Christians of ancient Corinth entertained some serious doubts about the importance of the resurrection and its impact on matters of life and death. Questions came up: Are the dead really going to be raised to life? How will that happen? If they are going to be raised, what will their bodies be like?

Saint Paul addressed the issues and answered the congregation's questions. He explained what would happen if the resurrection were removed from Christian faith: "If there is no resurrection of the dead, then not even Christ has been raised. And if Christ has not been raised, our preaching is useless and so is your faith" (1 Corinthians 15:13,14). The Corinthians were tugging on that resurrection thread, trying to pull it out, and their faith was getting a little frayed around the edges.

Commenting on Paul's words to the Corinthians, Luther wrote, "So all of this ties together, the apostles' Word and

Christ's Word, the belief and the profession of Christendom, and God's truth and majesty, so that one cannot give one the lie without involving the other."[1] He goes on to describe the connection between the resurrection and other articles of faith, comparing them to a chain in which every article is linked to another. With teachings so firmly intertwined, Luther understood that the denial of one important element of faith—Christ's resurrection above all—meant the chain would be broken and faith would be useless. Without the resurrection, Christ and all his words and works are a lie. "If you deny this article [the resurrection]," Luther commented, "you are not denying anything trivial, nor for that matter a single article, but you are actually giving God the lie to His face, saying: 'God is not God, Christ is nothing, etc.'"[2] Unraveling the garment of our cartoon character left him dizzy and bare. Removing the fact of the resurrection from the Christian faith leaves all Christendom in an equally pathetic state. Luther described that pathetic state like this:

> For if the resurrection is nothing and yet I believe in it, what is that but a mere dream [without] sequel? Then all of Christendom from the beginning of the world would have followed a false belief, and all would be poor, bewitched people who permitted themselves to be fooled and misled by an empty dream and phantom, one for which people had to endure every persecution, distress, and torture. And after hoping for and relying on this for a long time, they would have had to depart this life and die in that confidence and then find themselves deceived shamefully.[3]

Without Christ's resurrection, believers are left holding an empty dream, relying for a lifetime on a lie that ends in the final deception of death. Faith amounts only to a worthless idea—certainly a very pleasant idea—but still a worthless one. The resurrection becomes nothing more than an imagined event, unable to offer lasting hope and comfort in life or death. But Paul continued his lesson for the Corinthians, assuring them that "Christ has indeed been raised from the dead" (1 Corinthians 15:20). Like Paul, Luther knew that the truth of

Christ's resurrection replaced empty dreams and shameful deceptions with confidence in the face of death and with assurance in the hope of eternal life.

The thread of the resurrection runs back and forth through Luther's writings. It shows itself in places we would expect: Easter sermons, funeral sermons, comfort for the dying, and teachings about the Last Day. But it also surfaces in some less obvious places: in Luther's lectures on Genesis and discussions on the Sacrament, in preaching about the Word and the daily life of the believer. We will tug a bit on that thread (not so hard as to pull it out, of course) and follow it as it weaves its way through Luther's thought as a chief article of faith and a central element of salvation history.

In his writings, Luther presented the benefits of Christ's resurrection for each believer. He showed how it is central to the new birth of Baptism and its sustaining power for Christian life. For Luther, the hope of the resurrection provided assurance at life's end and new perspectives on death, burial, and the condition of the soul after death. The resurrection provides the sure hope of eternal life. Commenting on 1 Corinthians chapter 15, Luther wrote that "since every Christian must believe and confess that Christ has risen from the dead, it is easy to persuade him to accept also the resurrection of the dead; or he must deny in a lump the Gospel and everything that is proclaimed of Christ and of God. For all of this is linked together like a chain, and if one article of faith stands, they all stand."[4]

It is difficult to imagine that anyone who confesses Jesus Christ as Lord would want to rattle that chain of faith and deny Jesus' resurrection. Believers worship together each Sunday, "the first day of the week" (Luke 24:1), honoring the day of resurrection. We confess the words of the Nicene Creed, "He suffered and was buried. And the third day he rose again according to the Scriptures. . . . I look for the resurrection of the dead and the life of the world to come."[5]

The festival of Easter is celebrated with elaborate ceremony and great joy. But the thread of resurrection hope cannot be pulled out or we would fall victim to serious doubt or unbelief.

The most holy joy would simply evaporate in the face of life-threatening illness, grief over death, or even the common troubles and anxieties of daily life. At those times—that is to say, at all times—we need more than a weekly observance and a holy festival. The resurrection of Jesus Christ must be for us what it was for Luther: that all-important theme, a defense against despair and doubt, and the thread that holds together unsteady lives and shattered hopes.

Chapter 3

The Foundation, the Reason, and the Aim

On the way into church, a three-year-old girl told her mother what she had learned that morning in Sunday school. She explained how people stuck things in Jesus and made him bleed (the crown of thorns). The people hurt Jesus and put him on a cross and he died, and they put him in a dark place. Then she exclaimed (with both fists raised to show immense strength), "But Jesus had great power and he came alive again!"

No learned theologian could have recited the Gospel more clearly. The little girl knew the facts, and she knew what her Lord had done for her. In agreement with this three-year-old theologian, Luther argued for the importance of the simple facts of the story: "The best and safest is simply to stick with the words, just as they read, with childlike understanding."[6] He did not want human reason to tamper with the central truth of the resurrection; it was a message to be faithfully taught.

For Luther, there were two critical points concerning the Lord's resurrection: the facts and the benefits. In the first place, he said, we must know the history and events because "this article of faith on the resurrection is the chief one upon which our salvation is finally based, and without which all others would be useless and altogether fruitless."[7]

The second and more important point is the reason the facts are proclaimed—that the power, benefit, and comfort of the resurrection might be known. The hope of the resurrection doesn't come about through a simple knowledge of the facts. Satan knows the facts and receives no benefit from it. "For if we preach only its history, it is an unprofitable sermon, which Satan and the godless know, read and understand as well as true Christians; but when we preach to what end it serves it becomes profitable, wholesome and comforting."[8]

In the facts of the Easter narrative, we first learn the comfort of Christ's love for his disciples and for us. In spite of the earlier unbelief and denial of his disciples, the risen Christ greeted them as brothers. Luther remarked that Christ also dealt gently with Thomas and his doubts:

> This is written for our sakes, that we may learn how Christ loves us, and how amiably, fatherly, gently, and mildly he deals with us and would deal with us. With the godless and unbelievers who do not regard him at all, he is stern and severe. But he does not desire to overturn or reject the weak in faith, but bears patiently with their weakness, not snarling at them frightfully, but handling them gently and respectfully.[9]

In that account we find the assurance that Christ will confront our doubts and fears with gentleness. However, when doubts are not healed by the Word and are instead allowed to continue unchecked, the devil can gain a foothold in undermining our faith.

In 1538, Luther wrote "The Three Symbols or Creeds of the Christian Faith" to show agreement between the evangelical (Lutheran) doctrine and the teachings of the early church. In that work he explained that the devil attacks Christ on three fronts—denying his divinity, denying his humanity, and denying his work. Satan is not about to let such an important article of faith as the resurrection go untouched. Participating in Satan's attack on the work of Christ are those who refuse to believe that Christ rose from the dead and sits at God's right hand or anything else confessed about him in the creeds. "These," Luther explained, "will knock the bottom out of the barrel and put an end to the game. For therewith the whole

Christ will perish, and the world will think nothing of a future life. In that case Christ is nothing any more."[10]

The teaching of the resurrection must be firmly maintained. Luther stated: "Where this article, which forms the foundation, the reason, and the aim of all other articles of faith, is overthrown or removed, everything else will also topple and disappear with it. Therefore it is indeed necessary to foster and to fortify this article with diligence."[11] Saint Paul asked the Corinthian Christians, "How can some of you say that there is no resurrection of the dead?" (1 Corinthians 15:12). Luther felt it was shameful that the resurrection had come into question even in those early days of the church. If the resurrection is a lie, then all of God's promises are lies. Believers are left with only this earthly life and are, as Saint Paul said, "to be pitied more than all men" (1 Corinthians 15:19).

In Luther's opinion, the questions of the Corinthian Christians did not stem from simple curiosity but from outright doubt. Their questions "How are the dead raised? With what kind of body will they come?" indicated that they denied the bodily resurrection. Luther taught that the Corinthians accepted only a spiritual resurrection to new life and not the physical resurrection on the Last Day.

When doubts like this arise, other doctrines unravel. The Lord's Supper is called into question, since those who deny the fact of a physical resurrection may just as easily deny that Christ's body and blood are present in the Sacrament.

That line of reasoning in turn leads to doubt concerning Holy Baptism; if the Sacrament of the Altar is only bread and wine, then Baptism is only water and nothing more. For Luther, the validity of Baptism was tied to the promise of life found in the doctrine of the resurrection. To demonstrate the fact of the resurrection, Saint Paul spoke of the Corinthian custom of baptism on behalf of the dead. Luther commented on Paul's argument, "For it is incongruous, on the one hand to accept the validity of Baptism and on the other to reject a future life. . . . There is no pig, to say nothing of Christians, so stupid

11

as not to understand that Baptism serves no purpose if there is no resurrection."[12] The very practice of Baptism implies a belief in new birth and new life.

Further, this brings not only the sacraments but also Christ's incarnation and the virgin birth into question.

The denial of one mystery leads to the denial of others. Human reason is a definite gift and creation of God, but doubts about matters of faith come from trusting our own wisdom rather than the Word. Reason cannot imagine how God can physically raise those whose bodies have been burned to ashes, devoured by fish at sea, or decayed to dust.

However, if we believe that God is truly the Creator and is able to make things out of nothing, then we must also believe that he is able to raise the dead. The domino effect of doubt can only be countered by trusting the Word of God.

Commenting on the use of reason in approaching a doctrine such as the virgin birth, Luther wrote, "These articles of faith which we preach are not based on human reason and understanding, but on Scripture; it follows that they must not be sought anywhere but in Scripture or explained otherwise than with Scripture."[13] Luther had little patience with intellectual disputes concerning the Word. God provided other disciplines—grammar, rhetoric, philosophy, medicine—in which we can dig around, question, and argue. "But here with the Holy Scripture, the Word of God," Luther advised, "let disputing and questioning cease, and say, God has spoken; therefore, I believe. Here there's no room for disputation and argument, but rather, be baptized, believe on the woman's seed, Jesus Christ, true God and man, so that you might have the forgiveness of sins and everlasting life through his death and resurrection."[14] Approaching the resurrection with the question of "How is that possible?" only increases our distance from the truth.

Luther saw how Saint Paul set about preserving the truth of the resurrection and noted that the apostle was not willing to allow human reason to destroy the doctrine. Already in the opening verses of his resurrection chapter (1 Corinthians 15), Paul directed the Corinthians back to the Word, reminding them of the Gospel that had already been preached to them. Paul used two main points to support his arguments for the resurrection—first, the teaching was taken from Scripture, and second, many people were eyewitnesses of the event. Paul looked to Scripture, Luther wrote, "in order to resist (as I stated before) the temptation to take counsel with reason in this and other articles of faith, or to listen how the world with its wisdom presumes subtly to argue and to speculate about this."[15] If reason is consulted, then faith may be crowded out and the entire message mocked as foolishness.

To avoid doubt concerning the resurrection, Baptism, the incarnation, and every other doctrine, human reason must allow itself to be taken captive by the Word. On the road to Emmaus, Christ himself used the Scriptures to teach the disciples on the first Easter evening. Speaking on that text in a sermon for Easter Monday, Luther pointed out that it was the Holy Spirit, and not human reason, who interpreted the Word on that day when Jesus, beginning with Moses and the Prophets, explained to the disciples all that Scripture taught concerning himself.

There are few people, according to Luther, who really preach about the resurrection correctly. Those who argue so critically about the facts of the first Easter—Luther calls them "factious spirits"—will ultimately destroy the significance of those events and lose the person of Christ. For such people, Christ becomes little more than another visionary or prophet. To guard against such a loss, Luther warned, the resurrection is a subject that much be taught again and again. Then, of course, there will be those who mock and label presumptuous any preacher who claims the absolute truth of the resurrection along with all the doctrines of Scripture that follow it. These are the "factious spirits" again, and Luther warned that people will very likely rally to them:

> And as it is, the factious spirits enjoy two great advantages with the rabble: the one is curiosity, the other, satiety. These are two large gates through which the devil can pass with a wagon of hay, indeed, with all of hell, prompting them to say: "Oh, this man [the one who preaches the Gospel] can preach about noth-

ing but Baptism, the Ten Commandments, the Lord's Prayer, and the Creed, with which even the children are conversant. What's the idea, that he constantly harangues us with the same message? Who is not able to do that? After all, one must not always stick with the same thing, but develop and progress, etc." That signifies satiety with and weariness of the message.[16]

Progress, by definition, is a forward movement, but in matters of faith, the best "progress" is often a retreat back to the clear witness of God's Word.

Saint Paul wrote of Christ's death and resurrection according to the Scriptures. The risen Christ took his disciples back to Moses and the Scriptures. There in the Word we find the facts of the first Easter and all that Christ accomplished for us. Those who are bored with that message or curious to discover something new open the gates for the devil and his wagonload of doubt. Denying the facts of Easter leads to denying much more, but the faithful proclamation of Christ's resurrection—in all of its profoundly simple mystery—saves those who hear and believe the message.

Chapter 4

That by Believing You May Have Life

For Luther, the resurrection was the foundation of Christian faith; if that article is missing, other doctrines quickly come undone. The first critical point concerning the resurrection was the knowledge of the facts. The second point was an understanding of the benefits received through Christ's resurrection. What are those benefits? What exactly will the believer lose if the event of the first Easter is missing? Alister McGrath authored a book of insights into Christ's death, asking the title question, *What Was God Doing on the Cross?*[17] A similar question might be asked about the first Easter morning: Just what was God doing at the empty tomb? Martin Luther provided one possible answer to questions about the cross and tomb in a stanza of his Easter hymn "Christ Jesus Lay in Death's Strong Bands":

> It was a strange and dreadful strife
> When life and death contended;
> The victory remained with life,
> The reign of death was ended.
> Holy Scripture plainly says
> That death is swallowed up by death,
> Its sting is lost forever. Alleluia![18]

The thread of life and resurrection issuing from the empty tomb first wrapped itself around Calvary's cross. In the resurrection, the full power of the cross was revealed. Speaking about Luther's teaching on the two natures of Christ, scholar Marc Lienhard wrote: "The divine nature is hidden in the human nature, the cross hides the resurrection, weakness hides the power of God. This conception does not confuse the natures, but it is turned toward the future, toward the time when, by the resurrection and the proclamation of the Gospel, God himself will unveil the hidden realities in the incarnation and in the cross."[19] Medieval theologians often pointed to the cross of Christ as an example to be followed in human suffering. Luther differed from that view, looking to Christ not merely as an example but as the crucified and risen Savior to whom we must be united in faith. The cross was by no means the end of the story.

Luther liked to point out that it was Satan's terrible error, and his downfall, to imagine that the cross was the end. Here our single resurrection thread becomes an invisible trip wire, carefully buried under the cross, which triggers an explosive force against the devil when he kills the Savior. The satanic ambush failed when—in Luther's terms—Christ strangled the devil in his own body, drowned death in his blood, and erased sin with his suffering. In an Easter sermon, Luther described the trap set by the cross. Death and the devil imagined that killing Jesus Christ would be just like killing Lazarus or Isaiah or any other biblical figure. Satan thought to try his luck against Christ, not realizing that he was dealing with a very different target—the God-man, who had no guilt of his own for which to die. Luther described it this way: "But here death and the devil ran against a wall as they smash headlong against this man who could not die. He could not die because of his divinity, for it is impossible for God to die. Nor ought he to have died according to his human nature, for he had no guilt, and, therefore, death had no claim on him."[20] Satan blundered into what Luther called the "quiet strategy"[21] of Christ's death, wrongfully claiming a victim who did not deserve to die. Death and the devil simply could not hold on to this God-man.

In Galatians 3:13, Paul wrote, "Christ redeemed us from the curse of the law by becoming a curse for us." Commenting on

16

that passage, Luther said that Christ, of his own free will, became a curse, suffering death to set us free from death. Luther continued, "But because [Christ] was a divine and everlasting person, it was impossible for death to hold him. Therefore, he rose again on the third day and now lives forever; and there is neither sin nor death in him anymore, but only righteousness, life, and everlasting blessedness."[22] In his attack on Christ, the devil inflicted a wound, but he did not overpower him. Satan could attack only the Savior's human nature; he could not touch the Godhead.

In the resurrection, the tables were completely turned on death and the devil. Lecturing on Christ's work as our Redeemer and Deliverer, Luther said:

> For he not only redeemed us but also freed us rightfully for Himself, so that the devil and hell were compelled in strict justice to let Him go, because they had killed the innocent Son of God. Therefore the Law burned its fingers, and death dirtied its pants. The devil, death, and sin overreached themselves. There they all became guilty and debtors to God, to this Son Jesus Christ, who now has the right over against His enemies[23]

The conquerors (so they thought) became the conquered, and Christ's victory over the Law, sin, our sinful flesh, the world, the devil, death, and hell became the victory of every believer. Our weak human nature is quick to point out that it appears to be a doubtful victory—we still have to die. But according to Luther, Christ is the answer to physical death. He too was killed and laid in the grave, but death could not hold him, and death cannot hold us there either. Christians are free to throw the resurrection victory in the face of death and the devil with the taunt, "Do you remember how you devoured Christ? But you had to release Him, did you not? Indeed, He, in turn, has devoured you. Therefore you will also be unable to devour me, because I abide in Him and live and suffer for His sake."[24]

In his death and resurrection, Christ delivered us from death and the devil, won forgiveness of sins, and gave us his own righteousness. The resurrection is not just a sign of these things, but the actual granting of them. Commenting on the words of Romans 4:25: "He was delivered over to death for our sins and was raised to life for our justification," Luther said that Christ's death made satisfaction for sin and his resurrection brought us righteousness. He continued, "And thus His death not only signifies but actually effects the remission of sin as a most sufficient satisfaction. And His resurrection is not only a sign or a sacrament of our righteousness, but it also produces it in us, if we believe it, and it is also the cause of it."[25] Only this righteousness granted through the resurrection can save us. There is "no other righteousness," said Luther, "with which to pass muster before God."[26]

Our enemies, namely, sin, death, hell, and Satan, may still frighten and accuse us, but they cannot destroy us because Christ has given us his righteousness. When Luther preached the funeral sermon for Elector John of Saxony, he told the Elector's subjects that they must not look at the faults of their ruler. Instead, they should remember that Elector John "confessed Christ's death and resurrection, by which He swallowed up death and hell and all sins, and [their ruler] remained steadfast in this confession. This covers and swallows up the multitude of sins as the great ocean swallows a spark of fire."[27] Even though sin still remains in us, we are credited with righteousness for Christ's sake. We are carried along in God's mercy, Luther said, as long as we live in this life. Finally, Christ's resurrection will be realized in our own flesh when "the body of sin is abolished and we are raised up as new creatures on that great day. Then there will be a new heaven and a new earth, in which righteousness will live."[28]

Luther commented that a hungry person can be satisfied by bread and a miser with money, but only the teaching of the resurrection can satisfy Christians, because we know that only Christ and his righteousness can save us from God's wrath. Again in his funeral sermon for Elector John, Luther suggested this confident response to the devil's temptations of doubt and fear: "Devil, rage as much as you please, I do not boast of my good works and virtues before our Lord God at all, nor shall I despair on account of my sins, but I comfort myself with the fact that Jesus Christ died and rose again."[29]

The elevation of personal merit and works diminishes the work of Christ. Luther warned that those who try to overthrow the righteousness of Christ like this "are resisting the Father and the Son and the work of them both."[30]

In the resurrection just the opposite occurred; Christ rose from the dead and received us as brothers, uniting us to the Father. On the first Easter, Jesus told the women who came to the tomb, "Go and tell my brothers to go to Galilee; there they will see me" (Matthew 28:10).

Luther found a lesson in that simple sentence:

> These are the very first words they heard from Christ after his resurrection from the dead, by which he confirmed all the former utterances and loving deeds he showed them, namely, that his resurrection avails in our behalf who believe, so that he therefore anticipates and calls Christians his brethren, who believe it, and yet they do not, like the apostles, witness his resurrection.[31]

The benefits of the resurrection were freely given without any merit on the part of the apostles. They denied Christ and deserted him, hiding behind locked doors in fear for their own lives. Yet Christ didn't wait for a change of heart in his followers. He immediately called them brothers. In Christ's declaration of brotherhood, we have, without any merit on our part, one Father and one inheritance—the forgiveness of sins and a share in our Brother's eternal life and glory.

Another benefit of the resurrection comes through knowing Christ not only as our Brother but also as our King. The risen Christ is no longer bound by bodily, worldly things, like time and space. He is, Luther wrote, "to be recognized and believed in as one who through his power can reign everywhere, who can be present with us at all places and at all times, when and wherever necessary, and who will help us without being taken captive and hindered by the world and its power."[32] This new kingdom is not about temporal life and goods; its purpose is not found in teachings on marriage and family, how to build

19

and plant, how to rule a city or preserve world peace. The kingdom built on Christ's resurrection addresses the threats of
death, hell, and sin awakened by the Law. It is a kingdom that
shows us where we will be when this earthly kingdom has
passed away and we have left behind temporal life and possessions. It is a kingdom received by faith in the risen and reigning
King. This faith, Luther said, "is not an empty, dead thought on
the history about Christ, but that which concludes and is sure
that he is the Christ, that is, the promised King and Savior,
God's Son, through whom we are all delivered from sin and
eternal death; for which purpose he also died and rose again."[33]

Commenting on 1 Peter 1:3, Luther wrote, "We must preach
Jesus Christ, that he died and rose again, and why he died and
rose again, that through such preaching men might believe on
him and be saved. That is preaching the true Gospel."[34] What
was God doing at the empty tomb? Luther pointed to John 20:31,
in which the apostle writes that the facts of Christ's life, death,
and resurrection were recorded for one purpose: "These are
written that you may believe that Jesus is the Christ, the Son of
God, and that by believing you may have life in his name."

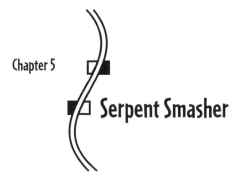

Chapter 5

Serpent Smasher

The apostle John told us that his Gospel was written so that
we might believe that Jesus is the Christ and have life in his
name. In much the same way, Saint Paul wrote in Romans 15:4
that God's Word was recorded for our benefit: "For everything
that was written in the past was written to teach us, so that
through endurance and the encouragement of the Scriptures
we might have hope." This hope is based, and was even in the
Old Testament, on the promise of life and resurrection through
Jesus Christ. For Luther, the thread of Christ's resurrection is
woven in and out of salvation history, from the first promise of
the Messiah recorded in Genesis, through the lives of the patriarchs, down to David's Son, who would inherit an eternal
throne and kingdom.

On the first Easter evening it was Christ himself who traced
the resurrection promise back to the Old Testament Scriptures.
Speaking to the two disciples on the way to Emmaus, "beginning with Moses and all the Prophets, he explained to them what
was said in all the Scriptures concerning himself" (Luke 24:27).
In Luther's opinion, Christ very likely began his lesson with the
messianic promise of Genesis 3:15: "I will put enmity between
you and the woman, and between your offspring [NIV text note:
"seed"] and hers; he will crush your head, and you will strike his
heel." Preaching an Easter Monday sermon on the Emmaus
account, Luther called these words of Genesis the "primary passage from Moses; and with this first promise, out of which all the

rest flow, [Christ] effectively and in richly spiritual manner pointed to his suffering and resurrection from the dead."[35]

Luther admitted that this first prophecy of the woman's Seed "is dark and impenetrable to human reasoning and the words are like flintstone and sharp thorns from which nothing can be squeezed."[36] But just as Christ opened the minds of the disciples to understand the Scriptures, his Spirit uncovers the meaning of the promise for us. Luther explained:

> From this [the first promise] an entire New Testament springs forth, all the discourses of Saint Paul and the apostles, who do not tell a great deal of the life and miracles of Christ, but where it is possible, use such a passage as a flower, so to say, with which to cover a great meadow, doing so by the aid of revelation and the Holy Ghost who knows how to grind and press the words thoroughly, so that they give forth the juice and power they possess.[37]

Far more than we can imagine flows from this promise of the woman's Seed.

The Holy Spirit reveals the meaning of the promise as well as the root of the problem for which the promise was given. The solution is difficult enough to understand, and human reason judges the problem to be equally absurd. Saint Paul explained in 1 Corinthians 15:21, "Since death came through a man, the resurrection of the dead comes also through a man." Luther commented that worldly wisdom sees this as a lie, this impossible idea that the entire human race has to die for the guilt of a single man. Even God's verdict in the matter is considered questionable, as Luther pointed out: "It seems too unfair and too absurd that God should treat this matter so strangely and take this silly position in His judgment. Because Adam bit into an apple, he is supposed to have effected that all men are doomed to die to the end of the world."[38] After all, Adam had not stolen anything or committed murder or adultery. How could one "apple" be so important, human reason asks, that so many excellent people— saints, prophets, and even God's Son—should have to die? The problem and the solution share some similarities. Luther explained that just as we die without any fault of our own because we are descended from Adam, we will live again without any merit of our own because of the death and resurrection of Jesus Christ. Adam's sin "becomes our own when we are born,"[39] and Christ's righteousness becomes ours in the new birth of Baptism. Luther wrote, "Just as Adam was the beginning, the first man, through whom we must all die as he died, so Christ is the first Man through whom we are all to arise to a new life as He arose first."[40]

Death entered the world through one man's sin. Yet from the beginning God took death captive so that he might use death itself to destroy death. The idea that God "appointed death to be the destroyer of death," Luther wrote, "can be gathered from the fact that He imposed death on Adam immediately after his sin as a cure for sin."[41] Luther said that this plan of death destroying death was similar to the situation in which the giant Goliath was beheaded by his own sword. Adam and Eve died, but they died in the hope of the resurrection through the promised Seed of the woman, who would with his own death defeat death. Along with Adam and Eve, we too have the hope of life in the midst of death, through the promised Seed, the Son of God, who crushed the serpent's head.

For Luther, the life and work of Christ, "this serpent smasher,"[42] were explained in great detail in the first promise. First of all, the passage shows that the child to be born, the Seed of the woman, is a true human being. No mention of a man is made in the promise, only that the Seed would be the child of the woman. This shows, Luther said, that the Seed would be "a natural human being of our flesh and blood but would not be conceived and born in sin like other descendants of Adam. He would be without sin and over him the devil would have no claim or power, and he would be able to crush the serpent's head."[43]

The promise of Genesis chapter 3 also indicated to Luther that the promised Seed would have to be true God, because only then would he have the power to crush the serpent's head and triumph over sin and death. Luther wrote that this passage

23

points out the clear hope of a certain resurrection and of renewal in the other life after this life. If the serpent's head is to be crushed, death certainly must be done away with. If death is done away with, that, too, which deserved death is done away with, that is, sin. If sin is abolished, then also the Law.[44]

All hope of victory is wrapped up in this promise of the woman's Seed.

Christ—the woman's Seed—would by his death and resurrection crush the devil's power. Similar verses throughout the writings of the prophets were related to the first promise. Through the work of the Spirit, wrote Luther, many later verses of Scripture can all be related to the Genesis promise, which expresses the meaning of all Scripture. Adam understood and believed this first promise, and Luther said, "From him this was transmitted to us all; just as he comprehended it, so it was passed from one to the other. It was preached and treated with ever growing clarity, from Adam to Abraham, from Abraham to Moses, David, etc., and thus to Christ and the apostles, from whom it came down to us."[45]

Luther followed the resurrection promise through the early chapters of Genesis. He summarized the progression in this way: "The burden of these first four chapters is that we should believe that after this life there is a resurrection of the dead and eternal life through the Seed of the woman."[46] In the first chapter, we see that man was made in the image of God, created for immortality. In the second chapter, mankind fell, through disobedience, from immortality to a state of mortality. In chapter 3, immortality is restored through the promised Seed. Even the murder of Abel in chapter 4 testifies to the hope of the resurrection, because after Abel was killed he still lived, since God bore witness to the fact that his blood cried out. "Therefore," Luther commented, "men have the hope of resurrection and a God who leads them out of bodily death to eternal life, who inquires after their blood as after something precious, just as the psalm also says (116:15): 'Precious is the death of His saints in His sight.'"[47] The thread continues through chapter 5 of Genesis as Enoch is taken into immortality without seeing death. With the story of

Enoch, Luther said that God gave to the ancient world the hope of a better life to come.

The promise of the woman's Seed and the promise that all nations would be blessed through Abraham's Seed were, according to Luther, both fulfilled on the first Easter. The Seed, or offspring, of Abraham is Christ, who took away the curse of sin and death. All nations would be blessed in Abraham's Seed, but they would not find the blessing within themselves or their own works. Luther spoke of being blessed in the Seed of Abraham "when I apprehend Him in faith; and the blessing clings to me in turn and permeates my entire body and soul, so that even the body itself is made alive and saved through the same Seed."[48] The blessing begins in this life with comfort and hope, to be followed later by resurrection to life on the Last Day.

The promise of life out of death is clearly found in God's command to Abraham to sacrifice his only son Isaac. Very little conversation is recorded between father and son, but Luther provided an additional script. He suggested that Abraham told Isaac that he was to be killed, and in reply Isaac pointed out that descendants had been promised through him. Luther imagined that Abraham's response went something like this: "God has given a command; therefore we must obey Him, and, since He is almighty, He can keep His promise even when you are dead and have been reduced to ashes."[49] There are strong contradictions in that scene—Isaac was to be the father of kings, yet he was to die without offspring. Only God's Word can reconcile those opposing ideas—he who lives will die, and he who is dead will live.

Luther said that the same contradiction is found in every Christian, for even though we are alive, we are considered dead because of sin, and even though we die, we will live in Christ. Facing death, we find ourselves in the same quandary experienced by Abraham and Isaac. We only see how life is taken away, not how it is returned. Luther recorded Abraham's possible thoughts on the matter:

Today I have a son; tomorrow I shall have nothing but ashes. I do not know how long they will lie scattered; but they will be brought to life again, whether this happens while I am still alive or a thousand years after my death. For the Word declares that I shall have descendants through this Isaac, even though he has been reduced to ashes.[50]

Abraham believed the doctrine of the resurrection and, in that belief, resolved the contradiction that cannot be resolved in any other way.

Luther suggested that Abraham and Isaac were able to mock death and regard it as sport, because they were so sure of the promise of life. This is an understanding that Luther called "the science of the saints,"[51] and expressed it in this way:

Let us have the same thoughts about our dead and about our bodies. This food of worms will not remain dust; but it will live again, because we hear Scripture saying that in the eyes of God death is some childish sport and is also such for all Christians, who believe in the God who gives life to the dead (Romans 4:17) and regards the deceased as living.[52]

Believers who have this understanding, Luther wrote, should give thanks to God for that knowledge. It is a "science" that each Christian must not only accept in theory but trust with his or her whole heart.

With the story of Abraham and Isaac, Luther also discussed the ram that took Isaac's place as a sacrifice. Luther had little patience with scholastic debates over questions such as "Where did the ram come from?" Those who truly believe in the Creator's power would not ask such questions, Luther noted, adding the sarcastic remark, "Evidently the only mistakes wise men make are enormous mistakes."[53] He repeated a Jewish legend that suggests the ram in the thicket had been created by God on the sixth day and miraculously preserved until the time of Abraham. Luther felt the story was a good one because it indicated a knowledge of the woman's promised Seed. In the legend Luther found Christ, destined from eternity to crush the serpent's head, appearing at the appointed time to become the sacrifice for all mankind.

26

Luther also included the First Commandment in his discussion of Abraham's faith. In that command "is contained the doctrine of faith and of the resurrection of the dead. 'I, the almighty Creator of heaven and earth, am your God; that is, you must live the life I am living.'"[54] If God is truly God, he is able to deliver us from all evils, including the evil of death. To deny God as Creator and Author of life is to deny the resurrection, and to deny the resurrection is to deny the Creator's power. Luther said that "in the First Commandment you will find Christ, life, victory over death, and the resurrection of the dead into eternal life, and finally the entire Old and New Testament."[55] The Creator is the God of Abraham, Isaac, and Jacob, and as Scripture teaches, he is the God of the living.

Luther followed the resurrection doctrine through the book of Genesis to the story of Joseph and Jacob in Egypt. Even though Joseph was raised to the highest rank in the land, he did not regard that fame as the greatest thing God had promised him. He looked for the greater promise of the life to come. Jacob, Joseph's father, approached death with confidence because he trusted in God. His belief was not, Luther said, just historical knowledge of God's actions, but faith in the promise, faith that honors God as truthful and believes in his Word. It is a faith that conquers death. In his discussion of Jacob, Luther included the story of Saint Agnes' martyrdom. As she was led to prison and torture, Agnes said she felt as if she were being led to a dance. Luther wrote that even though she was near death, she had "true wisdom and understanding, because of which she concluded that life was very close to her. Therefore she laughed at the devil and death and regarded them as a joke, because for her, death had been swallowed up through life. This is the theology we teach."[56] The confidence of Jacob and Saint Agnes may be shared by all Christians, Luther said, because even though death is near, we are baptized, we believe, and so we are alive and saved.

Luther found the resurrection in two Old Testament accounts to which Christ referred during his earthly ministry. When Moses lifted up the bronze serpent in the wilderness, Israelites who looked at the serpent were healed and lived. By this example, Luther said, we are to find comfort in temptation and in death, looking to Christ alone. In his wounds and death, we recognize our sin; and in his resurrection, we have victory over sin, death, and the devil.

The story of Jonah is also a picture of Christ and his resurrection. Christ came into the world and was devoured, as if by a large fish. Satan, death, and hell "swallowed" Christ when he was hanging on the cross, but it was impossible for them to hold him. He was "vomited up," that is, he came back to life, and what had been an opportunity for death became an opportunity for life. Lecturing on the book of Jonah, Luther said: "In this way death has become the door to life for us; disgrace has become the elevation to glory; condemnation and hell, the door to salvation. And this has happened through Christ, who was sinless."[57]

Luther found the resurrection theme in the Psalms. He understood the words of Psalm 45:6, "Your throne, O God, will last for ever and ever," to refer to the risen Christ. The ability to conquer death and claim an eternal throne is not something that can be done by a man or any other created being. Only God can create life, Luther argued, so Christ is true God, since he created life and destroyed death. In Elector John's funeral sermon, Luther quoted Psalm 116:15, "Precious in the sight of the LORD is the death of his saints." By that phrase, Luther said, we are to understand that when a saint dies, there is offered to God an "excellent, costly, precious sacrifice, the loveliest and sweetest odor of incense and the best and highest worship that can ever be given to him."[58] In Psalm 132:11, God promised David, "One of your own descendants I will place on your throne." Luther felt that Christ very likely used such a promise to teach the disciples on the road to Emmaus.

The risen, eternally reigning Son of David is Abraham's offspring, the promised Seed of the woman. The people of the Old Testament, Luther said, were saved by faith just as we are. Speaking of this faith, he wrote, "For if you believe that by this seed the serpent has been slain, then it is slain for you; and if you believe that in this seed all nations are to be blessed, then you are also blessed."[59]

Chapter 6

For You

A certain choir anthem has the simple, repetitious refrain "Jesus is mine, he is mine, he is mine."[60] At first glance, the text seems far too human-centered, pointing to what is "mine" rather than to Christ. But in his "Preface to the New Testament," Luther wrote that Christ must indeed become ours by faith. It is not enough to simply know the facts and events of his life. Luther said that the true, saving knowledge of the Gospel comes to us "only when the voice comes that says, 'Christ is your own, with his life, teachings, works, death, resurrection, and all that he is, has, does, and can do.'"[61] The woman's Seed has slain the serpent for us. The power and benefits of Christ's resurrection become ours when we know and believe that his victory was intended for us and given to us.

Christ died and rose again in his own person, Luther said, but we must become partakers in his suffering and resurrection; that is Christ's gift to us. In 1520, Luther composed words of spiritual comfort for the ruler of Saxony, Fredrick the Wise, who had become seriously ill. Luther directed Fredrick's attention to the personal nature of Christ's saving work. He wrote that Christ "is not only born to us, but also given to us (Isaiah 9:6). Therefore, His resurrection and everything He accomplished through it are mine. In Romans 8(32) the Apostle exults in exuberant joy, 'Has He not also given me all things with Him?'"[62] Concerning Luther's thought, Marc Lienhard wrote, "All that is said of Christ concerns the believer, and conversely, there is nothing in the life of the believer that is not based on Christ."[63] For Luther, the personal connection meant that Christ has justified those who believe. What was done by Christ was done not for himself but "for you."

This personal trust in Christ's saving work marks the difference between a basic understanding of the Gospel events and a living, saving faith in those same historical facts. It is not enough, Luther said, to see Jesus Christ only in the way that our eyes and senses might see him. To truly recognize him as Lord, we must see him as he is found in God's Word, as Luther commented:

> But when I come to understand the fact that all the works God does in Christ are done for me, nay, they are bestowed upon and given to me, the effect of his resurrection being that I also will arise and live with him; that will cause me to rejoice. This must be brought home to our hearts, and we must not merely confess it with our mouths.[64]

Historical knowledge examines the resurrection as if it were merely an interesting story. Faith looks at the same events with the understanding and trust that Christ's work was accomplished "for me."

Christ became our Brother, dying and rising again to restore us to a right relationship with his Father. Jesus shared our flesh and blood, confronting the Law, sin, and death on our behalf. Jesus said, "On that day you will realize that I am in my Father, and you are in me, and I am in you" (John 14:20). According to Luther's understanding, "that day" to which Christ referred is the day of his resurrection. The Son came from the Father, became one of us, and died to draw us to the Father. Luther described the benefits of this new relationship to the Father: "[Christ] forged these links between Himself and us and the Father, thus enclosing us in this circle, so that now we are in Him and He in us, just as He is in the Father and the Father is in Him. Through such a union and communion our sin and death are abolished, and now we have sheer life and blessedness in their stead."[65]

This union and communion is possible because Christ's saving work turned away the Father's wrath. Our sins are there—we feel them—but they are also not there because God, for Christ's sake, will not look at them. Discussing Christ's defeat of death and sin, Luther wrote that it is impossible for Christ with his righteousness not to please God. Enjoying that same righteousness by faith, it is also impossible for us not to please him. Luther said that Christ, in speaking of the Father, assures us, "[He] is no angrier with you than He is with Me; but if you know this and make it your own, you will also be certain that whatever you say, preach, live, and do will be right and good, yes, will be, and will be called, My own Word and work."[66] As the end of our lives approaches, we may wonder if those lives were pleasing to God. Then, by faith, each believer must see that his life is covered by the life of God's Son, with whom the Father is well pleased. Union with Christ provides confidence and assurance in the face of death.

Writing on the words of Psalm 45:6: "Your throne, O God, will last for ever and ever," Luther said, "God, however, cannot die, so neither can a humanity that is united to divinity die. Therefore everything this divine person takes hold of, everything that adheres to Him—this, too, escapes death, not by its own strength but by the favor of this divine person."[67] Our sin is great, but Jesus' death and resurrection are greater still. In the face of death, Luther said, "Swiftly fling out that defiance and boast, not of yourself or your righteousness, but of the fact that Jesus Christ died and rose again for you."[68] There is definitely a sequel to Jesus' resurrection. Saint Paul calls Christ the *firstfruits,* a description indicating that he is the first of many to enter the resurrected life. Our defiance grows out of the certain knowledge that we will follow the Savior through death into life.

With defiance comes boldness, even in the face of God's judgment. This boldness does not arise out of personal worth or courage but from the merits of Christ; merits and blessings so truly our own, it is as if we ourselves had won them. In his lectures on Galatians, Luther discussed the gift of Christ's righteousness and the rejection of personal worth before God.

The believer who enjoys Christ's righteousness must not entertain any notion of earning God's favor through personal merit. Commenting on Galatians 2:20: "I no longer live, but Christ lives in me," Luther wrote, "Christ and my conscience must become one so that nothing remains in my sight but Christ crucified and raised from the dead. . . . Considering only what I am and what I ought to be and what I am bound to do, I lose sight of Christ, who is my righteousness and life."[69] Jesus Christ died and was buried, and we will die and be buried. But Jesus rose from the dead and did not rise only for himself. Speaking of Christ as the firstfruits of the resurrection to follow, Luther said, "He also rose again for our sakes and made an exchange with us; as He was brought into death through us, we shall be restored from death to life through Him."[70] What Christ did, he did for all believers. What Christ did, he did for you. The shining thread of his resurrection has your name written all over it.

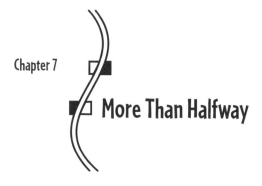

Chapter 7

More Than Halfway

God is at work in the waters of Holy Baptism, binding Christ's death and resurrection to our lives. Two important points are present in Luther's discussions of Baptism and the resurrection. First, he notes that an actual death and resurrection occur when we are baptized. We share Christ's death and are spiritually raised to life; all that remains to be done is the raising of our bodies on the Last Day. Baptism is, then, both death and birth. This leads to Luther's second emphasis, that Baptism is the beginning of a new life and the beginning of a journey through that life. It is a life of dying and rising that will take us to the fulfillment of the final resurrection when Christ returns.

In 1540, Martin Luther gave a sermon at the baptism of Bernhard Von Anhalt, the three-week-old son of Prince John. In his message, Luther described what God does in Baptism: "Is not this a beautiful, glorious exchange, by which Christ, who is wholly innocent and holy, not only takes upon himself another's sin, that is, my sin and guilt, but also clothes and adorns me, who am nothing but sin, with his own innocence and purity?"[71] God is at work in this glorious exchange, taking what Christ has done for us and making it our own. In Baptism the thread of the resurrection is wrapped around our lives. Luther wrote that even if there were not one death and one hell, but a thousand hells and a hundred thousand deaths, they would only be like tiny drops against the background of

Christ's victory. And, since we are baptized in Christ and believe in him, even thousands of sins, deaths, and hells would be nothing to us "because Christ's resurrection, victory, and triumph, which become ours through faith and baptism, are far greater."[72]

Baptism is deceptively simple in appearance. The water of Baptism, Luther said, is "real and natural water such as a cow may drink."[73] But through God's Word and the power of the Holy Spirit, that real, natural water becomes so much more. The outward ceremony of Baptism may differ according to tradition and practice. Water may be poured over the person to be baptized as a reminder of the spiritual washing that takes place, or the person may be completely immersed in the water. In his treatise of 1520, "The Babylonian Captivity of the Church," Luther wrote that he preferred full immersion because of the symbolism of death and resurrection in that practice. Immersion illustrates the fact that our sinful nature needs serious attention. Luther said, "The sinner does not so much need to be washed as he needs to die, in order to be wholly renewed and made another creature, and to be conformed to the death and resurrection of Christ, with whom he dies and rises again through baptism."[74] Baptism is not merely a symbol of dying to sin and finding a new opportunity to live a godly life. There is more, as Luther explained, "This should not be understood only allegorically as the death of sin and the life of grace, as many understand it, but as actual death and resurrection."[75] The baptized are included in Christ's death and resurrection and the sinner is fully and completely justified. Luther said that "a Christian is already more than halfway out of death. For his life on earth is nothing other than death; as soon as a Christian is baptized, he is thrust into death, as St. Paul declares in Romans 6:4."[76] Thrust into death, we are buried and raised with the One who promised, "Because I live, you also will live" (John 14:19). Baptism begins with death and ends in life.

While Luther may have preferred the image of death and life found in the practice of immersion, he did at times describe

Baptism as a washing. At the baptismal service for the infant Prince Bernhard, Luther said, "Therefore [baptism] also contains such strong salt and soap that, wherever it touches sin and uncleanness, it bites and washes it all away, eats and destroys both sin and death in an instant."[77] In the same sermon, Luther also said that Baptism "changes, cleanses, and removes the inherited disease of our impure and condemned birth from Adam."[78] The new life given in Baptism is both a future promise and a present reality. Luther explained that through Baptism we have spiritually risen from the dead; our souls possess their inheritance now and our bodies wait for the day of resurrection. Christ is our risen and ascended head, and because we are baptized in him, we are more than halfway to heaven. Luther said that "little remains for me to do but completely to remove the old skin, so that it too might again be renewed. For since the inheritance is already wholly mine, the husks and shells must then surely follow as well."[79]

Cleansed from sin now, we will on the Last Day rise to eternal life and enjoy complete righteousness in both body and soul. Baptism addresses the problem of our questionable parentage. Since we are descended from Adam and Eve, the sinful nature inherited from our first parents must be renewed by the power of the Holy Spirit. God delighted in his work of Creation, Luther said, and now "He takes pleasure in restoring this work of His through His Son and our Deliverer, Christ. It is useful to ponder these facts, namely, that God is most kindly inclined toward us and takes delight in His thought and plan of restoring all who have believed in Christ to spiritual life through the resurrection of the dead."[80] Those who are baptized, Luther noted, are adorned with the blood of Christ the Lamb, and Adam's children become new beings. Luther expressed faith's vision of this new life in a stanza of his hymn "To Jordan Came the Christ, Our Lord":

All that the mortal eye beholds
Is water as we pour it.
Before the eye of faith unfolds
The pow'r of Jesus' merit.

For here it sees the crimson flood
To all our ills bring healing;
The wonders of his precious blood
The love of God revealing,
Assuring his own pardon.[81]

The effects of Baptism are invisible to eyes of flesh, but not to eyes of faith.

A new life follows a new birth. In John 14:6, Jesus said of himself, "I am the way and the truth and the life." Speaking on this verse, Luther said that Christ is not simply an example to be followed in this new life; he is at our side, within us, and in our hearts. "This happens," Luther wrote, "when I believe staunchly in Him as the Savior who has passed through death unto the Father for me, in order to take me there too. Then I am on the right Way, the Way we must take and travel from this to the life beyond. This journey begins in Baptism."[82] The baptismal ceremony is over quickly, but the new life that begins there continues until we die. As long as we live, Luther wrote, we are continually dying and rising again until we enter eternal life: "We die, not only mentally and spiritually by renouncing the sins and vanities of this world, but in very truth we begin to leave this bodily life and to lay hold on the life to come, so that there is, as they say, a 'real' and bodily passing out of this world unto the Father."[83]

The daily baptismal experience is expressed by Luther in his Small Catechism, answering the question, What does such baptizing with water signify? "It signifies that the old Adam in us, together with all sins and evil lusts, should be drowned by daily sorrow and repentance and be put to death, and that the new man should come forth daily and rise up, cleansed and righteous, to live forever in God's presence."[84] The new birth in Baptism, Luther said, restores believers not so much to a life of hope as to a hope of life. Even though it is a life lived in the midst of death in this world, it is at the same time a life that will continue into eternity.

A Christian's entire life is a fulfillment of the Sacrament of Baptism, a continual dying and rising. Since we have risen to new life, we think and speak in a way that is different from the world around us. Since we are made new, everything we encounter in this life is seen and understood in a new way. Born first of earthly parents, we are born again, baptized into Christ's nature and kingdom. With new birth comes a new attitude toward those things the world finds frightening. This resurrection life, Luther said, means that a Christian can rejoice when things go wrong, knowing that "he is a mighty prince and lord when he lies in prison and superlatively strong when he is weak and sick, and that he is floating in honors when he is being covered with shame and ignominy."[85] If our journey through life brings suffering or ends abruptly in death, so much the better, to Luther's way of thinking: "The sooner we depart this life, the more speedily we fulfill our baptism; and the more cruelly we suffer, the more successfully do we conform to our baptism."[86] Life now is a prelude to the life to come. What we begin to see now through eyes of faith, we will see with eyes of flesh—risen and glorified—on the Last Day.

In Baptism the death and resurrection of Christ became our death and resurrection. With our lives intertwined with his life, we dare to go forward in confidence and hope through suffering and death into the final resurrection. And, as Luther said, we're more than halfway there already.

Chapter 8

That It May Be Fruitful in Us

Commenting on the fact that our baptismal journey may end suddenly and unexpectedly, Luther said, "If I persist in this faith and death attacks me . . . then the journey is over, and I am already at my destination as I leap into yonder life."[87] We know that our hope in Christ is not for this life only, and we look forward to the resurrection life to come. But God may not summon us immediately to leap into life. The baptismal journey may stretch across many years—a lifetime of dying and rising. At Baptism we are grafted into Jesus, the true vine, and through him we bear the daily fruit of his resurrection in our lives.

If the Gospel does not bear fruit, it is not the fault of the message. In that event, the blame lies with those who hear the Gospel but feel no need of its saving power. These people hear words but do not really pay attention to what they hear. Others hear and understand the message but do not change their lives or walk in the new life of Christ. Of this second category of listeners, Luther wrote, "They carry away only the words and prate much about them, but neither deeds nor fruit follow. The third class, however, are they that taste it and use it aright, so that it bears fruit in them."[88]

We find ourselves in that third category when Christ's resurrection is reflected in our lives. We bear fruit when we suffer as our Lord did and find in him courage in the face of suffering. We enjoy the peace and righteousness granted in Christ's victory, and with the assurance of our salvation comes the freedom to serve others.

Our journey through life is wrapped up in Jesus Christ, who called himself the Way, the Truth, and the Life. Using that reference from John chapter 14, Luther described the place of the Savior in our travels: "With a view to the beginning He is called the Way; He is the Truth with regard to the means and the continuation; He is the Life by reason of the end. For He must be all—the beginning, the middle, and the end of our salvation."[89] Baptized into Christ, we begin our journey. Walking with him means continual growth in faith. Finally, facing death with the risen Christ—who is the Life—we enter life.

A life intertwined with the life of Christ is no guarantee of an easy road—in fact, quite the opposite is true. Following Jesus means following him through suffering and death into the final resurrection. In John chapter 15, our fruitful connection to Christ is compared to a vine and its branches. Luther regarded the vineyard image as an especially delightful illustration and elaborated on the story with an entertaining dialogue between the vine and the vinedresser. In Luther's script, the vine catches sight of the vinedresser approaching with his clippers and—supposing it can speak—starts up this complaint:

> Ah, what are you doing? Now I must wither and decay, for you are removing the soil from my roots and are belaboring my branches with those iron teeth. You are tearing and pinching me everywhere, and I will have to stand in the ground bare and seared. You are treating me more cruelly than one treats any tree or plant.[90]

The vinedresser patiently explains to his agitated plant that he is working for the vine's own good. Useless branches must be pruned away so they do not suck out the strength and sap of the good branches. Pruning will cause the vine to yield a better crop. The situation proceeds smoothly until the vine gets a whiff of the fertilizer:

> Is it not enough that you are hacking and cutting me to pieces? Now with this filthy cow manure, which is intolerable in the

barn and elsewhere, you are defiling my tender branches, which yield such delicious juice! Must I stand for this too?[91]

We recognize in the unhappy vine our usual reaction to life's trials and our inclination in difficult times to regard God as unjust or uncaring. Yet in Luther's illustration God shows himself not as a tyrant but as a faithful heavenly vinedresser who cares for his vineyard and has no intention of ruining it. The world and its misfortunes, the devil, and even death itself are merely God's clippers and pruning hooks. Suffering and disgrace provide the fertilizer for the vinedresser's beloved vine. God will not let the pruning continue beyond what serves the best interests of the branches.

Luther explained that Christ used this image to illustrate his own suffering. Just as pruning caused the vine to yield richer fruit, Christ came into glory by way of the cross and death. Those who follow him, branches united to the vine, will share the same experience. The Father, our vinedresser, wants the vines to yield rich fruit; he loves his vineyard too much to let it grow without fertilizing and pruning.

Seen through this illustration, the suffering encountered in our journey through life takes on different meaning. God, the vinedresser, Luther said, reverses and renews all things, tending his vineyard with surprising commands:

"Death and grave, be life! Hell, become heaven and bliss! Poison, be precious medicine and refreshment! Devil and world, be of even greater service to My beloved Christians than the blessed angels and the pious saints!" For I can and will cultivate My vineyard in this way. All kinds of suffering and adversity will only improve it.[92]

With this insight, Christians face distress and even death with confidence. Luther added our response to his vineyard script: "All right, dear hoe and clipper, go ahead. Chop, prune, and remove unnecessary leaves. I will gladly suffer it, for these are God's hoes and clippers."[93] We will not always escape the pruning of trouble and grief, but we can be confident that these things are only evidence of the careful tending of our loving vinedresser.

Even the triumph of the first Easter did not allow the disciples to escape the pruning shears. Appearing to his followers as they hid behind locked doors, Christ removed the fear from his disciples' hearts, but he did not remove the outward danger. The disciples still had enemies, but inwardly, Luther said, they were changed. Having seen the risen Lord, they were filled with joy and boldness, fearless in the face of the hatred directed against them. Just as Christ came to his followers, God's Word comes to us and, by faith, Christ stands in our hearts, giving us the same courage. Then, according to Luther, we can declare, "My Lord Christ has by his resurrection conquered my need, my sin, death and all evil, and will be thus with and in me, so that body and soul shall want nothing, that I shall have all I need, and no evil shall harm me."[94]

The peace that Christ announced to his disciples on the first Easter was far different from the world's peace. Luther explained that worldly peace requires the removal of any outward evil disturbing that peace. In the presence of sickness or poverty, we expect a person to feel distress and fear. Only when these troubles are gone does the world grant its peace, but inwardly the person has not been changed. In opposition to this view, Luther presented a description of Christ's peace:

> Christian spiritual peace, however, just turns the thing about, so that outwardly the evil remains, as enemies, sickness, poverty, sin, death, and the devil. These are there and never desist, encompassing us on every side; nevertheless, within there is peace, strength and comfort in the heart, so that the heart cares for no evil, yea, is really bolder and more joyful in its presence than in its absence.[95]

However bold and fearless we hope to be, we are not always eager to face evil or death. Because our boldness may dissolve too quickly, we need to hear again and again the story of the first Easter. Christ's resurrection must be preached, Luther said, "to the end that it may be fruitful in us, quicken and kindle our hearts, and work in us new thoughts, new knowledge, new forces, life, joy, comfort, and strength."[96]

When we look at life through the cross and the tomb, we see that Christ shared our suffering; the vine endured the fate of its branches. Luther wrote that "Jesus Christ, God's Son, has by His most holy touch consecrated and hallowed all suffering, even death itself, has blessed the curse, and has glorified shame and enriched poverty so that death is now a door to life, the curse a fount of blessing, and shame the mother of glory."[97] We do not need to shrink from suffering and death because Christ so willingly embraced these things for our sake, and in doing so destroyed their power over us.

This good news is so immense that we cannot stuff it firmly into our hearts without some help. The Holy Spirit brings us this knowledge with the preaching of the Word, but trouble and suffering drive us to a more profound understanding of Christ's victory and its place in our lives. Perhaps a little unkindly, Luther compares our doubting hearts to a pig's bladder, which must be salted and stretched before it is useful. (He does not mention just exactly what it is useful for, but perhaps some things are better left unsaid.) Like the useful bladder, "this old hide of ours must be well salted and plagued until we call for help and cry aloud and so stretch and expand ourselves, both through internal and through external suffering, that we may finally succeed and attain this heart and cheer, joy and consolation, from Christ's resurrection."[98]

Suffering stretches us sufficiently to make room in our hearts for the Gospel, and trouble creates hunger for a message of hope. The devil may also try to use suffering and fear as tools, but only to drive us to despair. If that happens, Luther said, we are to rise up in faith and tell him, "Go away, Satan, and be quiet. My Christ lives."[99] As we have seen, the personal aspect of that defiance—my Christ—was important to Luther. An Easter hymn of his day stated the point correctly. The poet did not stop with the message "Christ is risen" but added the words "Let us all rejoice in this." Luther praised the writer and explained, "But how can we rejoice in it if we have nothing of it and it is not ours? Therefore, if I am to rejoice in it, it must be mine, that I may claim it as my own property, that it may profit me."[100] Here again Luther emphasized that living, fruit-bearing faith consists not just in knowing the facts but also in believing that God's Son suffered, died, and rose again "for me."

Luther gave the same personal importance to the gift of forgiveness. On the first Easter, Jesus commanded his disciples to preach repentance and forgiveness in his name to all nations. Luther expressed Christ's command in this way: "Forgiveness of sins is to be preached in my name, that is, for my sake, because I died for you and am risen from the dead; I gained forgiveness of all your sins through suffering, dying, and resurrection, and present it to you as a gift."[101]

The gift of forgiveness means that we are no longer enslaved by the Law, as Saint Paul wrote in Galatians 2:19, "Through the law I died to the law so that I might live for God." Commenting on that passage, Luther described the Law as a grave that holds us captive. Just as Christ's grave was found open and empty, the tomb of the Law must release its grip on us. Luther said, "Hence the Law is now empty; and I have escaped from my prison and grave, that is, from the Law. Therefore the Law has no further right to accuse me or to hold me, for I have risen again,"[102]

Even though we are free, the backward pull is still strong. As we struggle daily with sin, our fallen nature makes every effort to drag us back into the grave of the Law. As Luther put it, "You may tie a hog ever so well, but you cannot prevent it from grunting."[103] This daily wrestling match will continue until the Last Day, when there will be no more need for forgiveness. The Holy Spirit works in us, Luther said, daily granting forgiveness until the resurrection finds its final fulfillment and we become "perfectly pure and holy people, full of goodness and righteousness, completely freed from sin, death, and all evil, living in new, immortal, and glorified bodies."[104] Buried with Christ in Baptism and spiritually raised again, we have been reconciled to God. We no longer need to be consumed with ourselves or with efforts to earn God's favor—we are free to serve our neighbor in love. The fruit of the resurrection in our lives is granted for the benefit of others. In Luther's words, Christ instructs us, "I shall communicate to you My purity, holiness, death, resurrection, and all that I can do. Therefore you should let My love for you be reflected in your love for one another."[105] The risen Christ told his disciples, "As the Father has sent me, I am sending you" (John 20:21). The good news of forgiveness, of the peace and joy found in the empty tomb, must be boldly shared. The thread of the resurrection, woven into our lives, firmly tamped down by suffering, courage, and service, must be used to draw others in as well.

Chapter 9

Faith Lives upon No Other

In Baptism we are taken into the life of Christ, the vine. His resurrection is wrapped around our lives as we are raised up to begin a lifetime of dying and rising. God not only begins the new life within us but also provides the means by which that life is nourished. The resurrection life is sustained as the risen Christ comes to us in the Sacrament of the Altar and the preaching of the Word.

In their sustaining power, Baptism and Holy Communion provide both medicine and poison. Medicine prescribed by a doctor is beneficial to the patient precisely because it is a poison that destroys the bacteria or virus that's causing the fever or illness. Luther understood death—defeated and rendered powerless in Christ's resurrection—as this medicine and poison. The poison of the empty tomb destroys the poison of death. Luther said, "Thus we have drunk a salutary medicine in Baptism and the Sacrament, which expels and removes our poison. This does not kill me but the very enemy who intended to kill me with it."[106] Modern medicine provides useful examples to illustrate Luther's thoughts. The venom of a poisonous snake is used to produce the serum that serves as the antidote for snakebite. A vaccine to prevent a disease like polio is produced from a "killed" form of the disease-causing virus. By his death, Christ destroyed death's power and conquered Satan, who wielded death as a weapon against us. Death was transformed from a curse into a cure. Death is, Luther said, "a real divine antidote, not taken from a physician's pharmacy but prepared by heaven and given to us through Christ's resurrection. It will be harmless for us, but it will kill and ruin only him who gave and served us this poison."[107] The "killed virus" of death is administered to us through Baptism, the Sacrament of the Altar, and the proclaimed Word. Through the cross and empty tomb, death becomes deadly to death and serves as life-giving medicine for us.

For Luther, the Lord's Supper was not only medicine but nourishing food as well. In the Sacrament, Christ gives his body and blood to sustain faith and provide food for bodies that will one day be raised to life. Eternal food provides nourishment for eternal life. The doctrine of the Lord's Supper was one topic debated by Lutheran and Reformed theologians at the Marburg Colloquy in 1529, an effort to bring about political unity through religious agreement. The relationship between the eternal food of the Sacrament and the hope of the resurrection was one point of discussion. The Reformed argued that the hope of the resurrection is taken away if the bread of the Lord's Supper is said to be the body of Christ. If Christ's risen and glorified body is confined in earthly elements, no promise remains for our bodies of flesh on the day of resurrection.

Taking the opposite stance, Luther argued that the promise of the resurrection was actually supported and confirmed by the teaching of Christ's presence in the Sacrament. The Word of God states that Christ has a body, that his body was raised, and that he ascended to sit at the right hand of the Father. The Word of God also states that Christ's body is given to us in the Supper. In Luther's understanding, if the Word says that Christ is raised to the right hand of God, then he is; if the Word says that the bread is the body of Christ, then it is. Concerning the words "This is my body," Luther stated, "This I also believe because my Lord Jesus Christ can easily do this if he desires to and in his words he testifies that he does desire to do it."[108]

Luther spoke of his firm belief in the eternal food of Christ's body and blood in his Easter hymn "Christ Jesus Lay in Death's Strong Bands":

Then let us feast this Easter Day
On Christ, the bread of heaven;
The Word of grace has purged away
The old and evil leaven.
Christ alone our souls will feed;
He is our meat and drink indeed;
Faith lives upon no other! Alleluia![109]

In the sacraments and in the resurrection, as in all other articles of faith, the Word of God must be trusted above the arguments of human reason and the evidence of human senses.

The message of comfort and joy experienced by the apostles on the first Easter was a message to be proclaimed to the world. After his resurrection, Christ saw to it that his church would be nourished not only by the sacraments but also by the preaching of the Word. In Luke 24:46,47, he told his disciples, "This is what is written: The Christ will suffer and rise from the dead on the third day, and repentance and forgiveness of sins will be preached in his name to all nations, beginning at Jerusalem." Speaking on that text, Luther again stressed the importance of knowing the personal benefits found in the resurrection. In Christ's name "pardon for sins is to be preached, which he obtained through his suffering and resurrection, so that whoever would have forgiveness of sins should believe that Christ suffered and rose again from the dead for him. That is the true kind of preaching."[110]

The office of preaching is not limited to a recitation of the events of Christ's life. Christ gave his disciples authority in his name over Satan and the powers of hell and commanded them to preach forgiveness of sins. In John 20:21, Jesus commissioned his followers: "As the Father has sent me, I am sending you." Commenting on that passage, Luther said, "With this Christ entrusts to his disciples the office of proclaiming the Gospel, telling of and applying Christ's suffering and resurrection according to their intended purpose. For if the suffering and resurrection of Christ had remained apart from the office of preaching as a mere narrative or history, it would have been an exercise in futility, of no use to anyone."[111]

In another sermon on the same text, Luther explained that the words that Christ left behind are so powerful that when we speak them, it is as if Christ himself speaks. Far from being an exercise in futility, the Gospel message saves those who hear and believe it. Luther explained, "And this is the power we have from his resurrection and ascension; there he gives us power to kill and to make alive, to consign to the devil and to rescue from him."[112]

Luther was aware of the possibility of complaints concerning the repeated preaching of the resurrection. Having heard the story a few times, believers begin to feel that they know the facts pretty well and don't really need to hear it all again. Luther himself voiced that concern in a sermon on Easter Tuesday, knowing that his listeners had been hearing the Easter narrative for several days during that season. The teaching of the Gospel isn't based on human preference (we've been warned already of the devil's double gates of curiosity and satiety) but on the command of Christ. Luther said, "I think, beloved, you have heard enough in these days on the resurrection of Christ, what it works, why it came to pass, and what fruit it bears. But since the Lord commanded those who preach the Gospel to be steadfast and diligent in this proclamation, we must dwell upon it ever more and more."[113]

The continual repetition of the Gospel message may lead some people to consider the good news as "insignificant and as nothing more than a message characteristic of a child,"[114] yet in the childlike simplicity of that message is contained the whole mystery of the kingdom of heaven. In the Gospel we learn how Christ in his own body blotted out the sins of the world, how he defeated death and ascended to reign in power, and how he commanded that this message should be proclaimed so that all who believe will share his victory. Luther exclaimed, "Would to God this were a doctrine and knowledge as insignificant and trivial as they consider it to be!"[115]

As an ambassador of Christ, Luther said, it is not the preacher's task to teach about home economics, agriculture, or nutrition. For those matters God provided our own reason and plenty of people skilled in temporal affairs. Just as our hope in Christ is not for this life only, the preaching office reaches far beyond the limits of this life. Speaking on that office, Luther wrote: "Our only concern is to teach how—after Baptism—we may get from this to yonder life."[116]

Luther noted that even though believers exercise the powerful authority of Christ's message of life and forgiveness, it is still Christ's authority. We have the command to teach the words of eternal life, but we cannot create faith in those words. Only God can give that growth. The preaching of the Gospel is a service rendered, a treasure given to others in the name of Jesus Christ. After his resurrection, Christ did not reject his disciples because of their weakness and denial; he patiently taught them the words of life. The risen Christ is a model for ministry, Luther said, and we should use our gifts to serve and instruct the weak, patiently teaching them "until they are grown and can stand on their own feet."[117]

The living Lord is present and active in the ministry of those who proclaim his Word. Luther expressed this thought: "Christ has established through his resurrection that whenever a called servant of the Church, or someone else in time of need, absolves his neighbor who is distressed and desires comfort, it shall count as much as if Christ had done it himself, because it was done at his command and in his name."[118]

As we wait for the day of resurrection, God uses the death-dealing poison to destroy Satan's power and the life-giving medicine of the Gospel to bring us to life. We die daily and rise to walk with Christ, sustained and nourished by the good news of Christ's resurrection, fed to us in Word and sacrament.

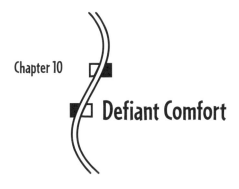

Chapter 10

Defiant Comfort

A recent news article on American attitudes toward end-of-life issues noted a change. Instead of dying at home, many people now face death in hospitals or nursing homes. Medical research gives doctors more weapons in the fight against terminal illness but leaves them ill equipped to face the losing battle of death. The author of the article commented, "Dislodged by modernity, dying became a taboo, slightly gross subject for polite conversation. Physicians and the families of their patients began to see death as a defeat, not an inevitable culmination."[119]

For Martin Luther, death—viewed through eyes of faith—is certainly inevitable, but it is not something ordinary or natural. Mankind has a tendency to view death as the natural end of life, as natural a process as the rising and setting of the sun. Luther took a different and more serious point of view: "Scripture teaches us that our death and dying does not come in a natural way but that this is a fruit of and the penalty for our father Adam's sin. He offended the Sublime Majesty so outrageously that he and all who are descended from him and are born on earth must die eternally."[120] Life is a journey toward death. In one sense, a person who contracts a deadly, infectious disease begins to die from the moment of infection. Because we are infected by inherited sin, Luther said, we also begin to die "right from our mother's womb."[121]

In 1 Corinthians chapter 15, Saint Paul refers to death as "the last enemy to be destroyed" (verse 26). All of the other enemies—and for Luther these others were our sinful flesh, the world, the Law, and sin—end at death. Death is not simply an event at the end of life. It is the greatest and last enemy because it is the one that survives all other enemies and holds us captive. The people of the world ignore death or try to and, in Luther's terms, "run to their grave backwards"[122] until they fall in. They may ignore the last enemy, but they cannot escape from it.

For Luther, it is in the face of this inevitable, overpowering enemy that the theme of the resurrection comes into its own. There is a defeat involved, but through Christ, it is death that becomes the conquered victim. A Christian, Luther said, is already thrust into death by the fact that he or she has become a Christian. In a current figure of speech, a person described as having "one foot in the grave" is usually viewed as one who is near death due to age or illness. Luther used the same image to describe instead the Christian's nearness to life, because Christians face death with the risen Christ beside them. Luther wrote:

> However, [the Christian] enjoys the advantage of already being out of the grave with his right leg. Moreover, he has a mighty helper who holds out His hand to him, namely, His Lord Christ; He has left the grave entirely a long time ago, and now He takes the Christian by the hand and pulls him more than halfway out of the grave; only the left foot remains in it.[123]

Christians do not need to ignore death and run backward to their graves. From Luther's point of view, we have already been in our graves and are on the way out! In spite of the fact that we are climbing out of the grave, death has not yet gained status as a popular subject for polite conversation. Even with confidence in Christ, the thought of death fills us with fear. Emotions may cause our faith to swing like a pendulum between confidence and despair. In Luther's thought, fear of death is Satan's handiwork. The devil leads us into fear and worry by causing us to look closely at "the gruesome mien and image of death."[124] In his efforts to restore death to its place as the final victor, the devil also turns our attention to God's

wrath over sin. Satan tempts us to doubt God's forgiveness and
to imagine that our lives are beyond the reach of God's grace.
The same fearful images assaulted Christ as his enemies
mocked him on the cross with the challenge "Save yourself!"
At death the devil taunts us with the question, How have you
lived? and tries to terrify us with the thought that we dare not
stand before God. "In that way," Luther said, "he fills our foolish human nature with the dread of death while cultivating a
love and concern for life, so that burdened with such thoughts
man forgets God, flees and abhors death, and thus, in the end,
is and remains disobedient to God."[125]

When we are so caught up in fear, Luther said, "nobody
believes that God has commanded confidence and has condemned despair."[126] Speaking of the fear and uncertainty of
death, Luther wrote, "Even the saints dreaded it, and Christ
submitted to it with trembling fear and bloody sweat (Luke
22:42-44). Therefore, in no other area has divine mercy been
more concerned about comforting faint hearts than in the matter of this evil, as we shall see below."[127] Luther continued,
"God has ordained that this evil be brought to an end by death,
and that death be the minister of life and righteousness."[128]
Having shared, through Christ, our terror of death, God stands
ready in that moment to provide his greatest comfort.

As much as we might wish to hang on to this hope and
comfort, it slips away all too easily in the face of the devil's
temptations. Sometimes, in Luther's words, God "steps
behind the wall a bit,"[129] hiding his presence from the feeble
sight of our faith. Even though our teachings are full of the
good news of Jesus' death and resurrection, we lack the
strength to hold on to the promise. God himself preserves us
in faith. In his last sermon, given in Eisleben in 1546, Luther
spoke of the God-given peace available for us. Luther states
that Jesus has promised us, "If evil befalls you, I, the Christ,
will give you the courage so that you will even laugh about it
all, and the pain shall not be so great for you, and the devil
not so bad. Even if you walked on live coals, you will have the
feeling that you walk on roses."[130]

God helps us look behind the terrifying mask of death to see that it is harmless to us. Death's appearance is that of a poisonous snake that has already been killed. The snake may still look frightful, but it can no longer cause any injury. We must look beyond the frightening images and leave behind the burden of a conscience consumed with guilt. Comfort comes, Luther wrote, with this knowledge: "[Christ] poured out His life and spent it lavishly for me. When I feel your terrors and threats, O Law, I immerse my conscience in the wounds, the blood, the death, the resurrection, and the victory of Christ. Beyond Him I do not want to see or hear anything at all."[131]

We would do well to immerse ourselves in Christ's work before the approach of death. In his book *The Troubled Dream of Life,* author Daniel Callahan asks, "How might we try to think about death in our lives? What should it mean to us, and what kind of persons should we try to become as we approach our end? How ought we to bear pain, suffering, and fear?"[132] Luther agreed that such questions should be addressed early on—at the moment we face death we are not able to address those issues effectively. In his "Sermon on Preparing to Die," Luther wrote, "We should familiarize ourselves with death during our lifetime, inviting death into our presence when it is still at a distance, and not on the move."[133] Luther was more than willing to drag death back into the arena of polite conversation, as long as the risen Christ was included in the discussion.

In our thoughts and conversations, we are horrified, yet somehow fascinated, with the fearful images and experiences surrounding death. Satan would very much like to have us focus on those things as we sink into guilt and fear. To avoid that temptation, Luther advised some practice in advance of life's end: "You must look at death while you are alive and see sin in the light of grace and hell in the light of heaven, permitting nothing to divert you from that view."[134] We must not wait until death to adopt a new perspective. The Israelites learned to turn away from their own wounds to look at the healing bronze serpent, and we have to tear our eyes away from our sin and guilt. In order to defeat death, we must cling to death's destroyer. We must look only at Christ, at his death and resurrection, in order to find life and healing.

In Christ all things have been made new, and even death—having lost its power to hurt us—is something entirely different. Including Christ in the discussion means to look at death with his eyes, hear about it with his hearing, and understand it with his mind and heart. In his funeral sermon for Elector John, Luther gave instruction on this new view of death, comparing the eyesight of unbelief to the empty and unmoved vision of a cow:

> Hence, one must look upon a Christian death with different eyes, not the way a cow stares at a new gate, and smell it in a different way, not as a cow sniffs grass, by learning to speak and think of it as the Scriptures do and not considering deceased Christians to be dead and buried people. To the five senses that is the way it appears.[135]

Leaving our cow-eyed point of view and adopting Christ's eyesight gives us a new image of death. Because Christ's death destroyed death, that which we fear so much can now be understood simply as sleep.

Luther thought of Jesus' death as a "real" death. Our struggle with the temptations of doubt and denial, the suffering inflicted by unbelievers, dying and rising in Baptism—these things Luther considered "real" deaths. Luther considered physical death as a childish death or an "animal death."[136] The "real" deaths were matters of great importance. Falling asleep in Christ, our "animal death," was not a death to be greatly feared.

Luther used the experience of physical birth to present another way of looking at physical death. An infant passes in danger and pain from the security of his mother's womb to life in a world that is immense by comparison. In the same way, a person leaves this present life, often in suffering and pain, through the narrow passageway of death. Accustomed to our present, expansive, and familiar home, we are afraid of the apparent darkness waiting for us. Luther explained that "although the heavens and the earth in which we dwell at present seem large and wide to us, they are nevertheless much narrower and smaller than the mother's womb in comparison with the future heaven."[137] The new home waiting for us is far greater than we can imagine, as far beyond our understanding as the immense size of this present world is beyond the grasp of the unborn child.

From another point of view taken from Scripture, Luther saw death as a journey. It was a way of "proceeding," of going from this life to the next. When a person is lying on his deathbed, Luther explained, "Then, too, a road stretches out before him that he must walk. He cannot tarry here but must travel a way that he cannot see, on which his feet cannot tread, on which he cannot travel by wagon. Yet one commonly says: 'He is departing; he is gone.' "[138] Even in this unknown journey there is assurance, because Jesus called himself the Way. The Christian is always prepared whenever this journey begins, because he has already shared Christ's death and resurrection in Baptism.

Speaking of the journey's end, Luther elaborated on Jesus' words "I am the way and the truth and the life":

> I will be the Bridge to carry you across. In one moment you will come out of death and the fear of hell into yonder life. For it is I who paved the way and the course. I walked and traversed it Myself, so that I might take you and all My followers across. All that is necessary is that you unhesitatingly set your foot on Me, wager boldly on Me, go cheerfully and happily, and die in My name. [139]

Fellow believers may give comfort and encouragement as death approaches, but each Christian must face the last enemy alone and step onto the "bridge" alone. Luther wrote, "Each one must see to his own redoubt and engage the enemies, death and the devil, in combat himself and come to blows with them all alone. Then I shall not be with you, and you will not be with me."[140]

At death, when no human help is possible, each believer must cross the bridge. Our fearful imagination tells us that we are entirely alone, but that is not the case. Luther explained: "You think you are forsaken by God and everybody, yea, you imagine how God and everything are against you. Then you must restrain yourself to quiet and cling only to God, who must deliver you."[141] Jesus Christ successfully faced death and the devil and traveled from death into life, becoming both the bridge and the one who carries us across.

Fear and doubt shake the grasp of our faith, but Christ will not release his hold on us. In moments of weakness and terror, we experience the greatest comfort and the most profound lesson in faith, as Luther pointed out:

> [Faith] is a high art and a lesson which no saint has been able to master or fathom unless he has been in despair, in the anguish of death, or in extreme danger. For there one sees that faith overcomes sin, death, and hell. These are no ordinary enemies; they make you sweat, crush your bones, and make heaven and earth too confining for you. At such a time there is no one who could help you but this Person alone, who says: "It must be I who dare not lose you. This is the Father's will."[142]

When we are face-to-face with death, we need to remember Christ's strong grip. Our senses record the sights and sounds, and our emotions react to the evidence and experiences surrounding death. The Word may take a backseat to reason in an emotional storm that is not unlike our daily experience with sin. We certainly know and believe that Christ shed his blood for us, but we still struggle with sin and guilt. We wonder if our sins are really forgiven. In such circumstances, Luther said, we are to hold on to the Word and promises of God:

> But over against all that reason suggests or tries to fathom and explore, yes, against everything that all senses feel and comprehend, we must learn to adhere to the Word and simply to judge according to it, even though our eyes behold how man is interred, furthermore, that he decays and is consumed by worms and finally crumbles into dust. Likewise, even though I feel sin oppressing me so sorely and my conscience smiting me, so that I cannot ignore these, yet faith must conclude the opposite and hold firmly to the Word in both these instances.[143]

God's Word tells us that Jesus Christ is able to help us in death and in life. It is a Word to be trusted.

Advance preparation in spiritual matters is an important aspect of learning to die in faith, but Luther also gave advice on settling the practical, temporal issues that come up in the business of dying. In this he turned to the example of the Old Testament patriarchs. They were saints who displayed a firm faith in the resurrection of the dead, yet they were careful to take care of their worldly affairs before death. Concerns of land and inheritance were set in order so that no quarrels would come up between family members. Looking to the example of Jacob as he gave gifts of land to his sons, Luther wrote, "Thus before a godly head of a household departs from this life, he sets everything in his house in order. He wants some things to be given to his wife and some things to his son and daughter. For he thinks: 'These things have been entrusted and committed to me by God. I am disposing of them with composure and confidence.'"[144]

In his "Sermon on Preparing to Die," Luther gave similar counsel—the dying person should set his temporal affairs in order so that there are no arguments among his survivors. The one facing death should also take spiritual leave of others, that is, he should forgive people who have offended him and seek forgiveness from those whom he has offended. He should turn to the sacraments to find spiritual strength as he nears death. Even the funeral service has special purpose—that God's Word should be proclaimed to glorify him and strengthen the faith of his people. We are to give thanks to God, more ready to praise his grace and mercy than to fear death. Luther commented, "Love and praise make dying very much easier . . . to that end may God help us."[145]

Dying is not so easy or our faith so great that we can avoid the sorrow it brings. Unbelievers—and sometimes believers as well—try to establish the absence of grief as a virtue. That attitude, Luther said, "is an artificial virtue and a fabricated strength, which God did not create and also does not please him at all."[146] God created us with emotions and would not have us deny them. At the funeral for Elector John, Luther gave this counsel to his congregation:

> For the steadfast man is not the one who thinks himself so strong that he refuses to be touched when a good friend has slipped away; rather the Christian is one who is hurt but yet endures it in such a way that the spirit rules the flesh. For God has not created man to be a stick or a stone. He has given him five senses and a heart of flesh in order that he may love his friends, be angry with his enemies, and to lament and grieve when his dear friends suffer evil.[147]

It is not the avoidance of grief and fear but the enduring of them that matters. Luther recognized that fear of death is natural; death is, after all, a penalty for sin. He said, "I do not like to see people glad to die. I prefer to see them fear and tremble and turn pale before death but nevertheless pass through it."[148] Grief over death can be faced when seen through the framework of Christ's death, a death that rendered death harmless to us.

Our attitude of hope in the mysterious issues of death and eternal life should mirror our view of more simple, temporal matters. "Would to God," Luther wrote, "I could muster such hope of the resurrection from the dead as a farmer musters hope from a grain of wheat."[149] Ordinary human hope is deceiving because it lacks the certain promise of resurrection and life. But even that shallow hope, Luther said, is a gift from God, given to prevent crushing despair. Such feelings serve as a reminder of the real hope found only in Christ.

If grief and hope can be transformed by faith, then perhaps a certain amount of Christ-centered cheer is also possible even in the face of death. A poem of Luther's day expressed an uneasy and slightly silly sort of peace:

> I live. How long, I do not know;
> Must die, but know not when I'll go;
> Pass on, but know not where 'twill be.
> My cheerfulness surprises me.[150]

A Christian who knows Christ as the Way, the Truth, and the Life knows exactly where he is going. With this in mind, Luther cheerfully reversed the verse:

> I live. How long 'twill be, I know;
> I die; know how and when I'll go
> (namely every day and hour before the world);
> Pass on, and know, praise God, where to.
> Why should I now be grieving so?[151]

The hope of the resurrection enables us to endure grief. People who are already climbing out of their graves enjoy a decidedly different point of view than that of the rest of the world. Suffering and death can be faced head-on with the cheerful sort of confidence found only through faith in Christ.

Luther goes beyond good cheer to recommend an attitude of stubborn defiance towards death, sin, or whatever Satan may throw at us. We know what is ahead for us, and it is not what the devil has planned. Luther wrote, "Therefore we who have now reached the end of the world have the defiant comfort that it will be but a little while, that we are on our last lap, and before we are aware of it, we shall all stand at Christ's side and live with Him eternally."[152]

Satan has an overwhelming desire to destroy Christians, hoping through death to snatch them from Christ. The enemy will find that his appetite cannot be satisfied. Luther challenged the devil to go ahead and devour Christians, adding, "For you will not find what you are seeking and desiring, and that is the best and greatest part of us, indeed, our whole life and treasure, namely, this article of the resurrection in Christ."[153] This great treasure of life and resurrection cannot be taken from us because it rests "in safe custody"[154] in the hands of Jesus Christ. He is the firstfruits, the first to rise from the dead, and in his resurrection is the promise that we will also rise—much to the disappointment of Satan's insatiable appetite. Death and sin are enemies that frightened even the mightiest of saints, but now they have been swallowed up in victory.

The source of our defiance is Jesus Christ, who defied death on our behalf. As the hour of his death approached, Jesus told his disciples, "Because I live, you also will live" (John 14:19). For Luther even those few words indicated Christ's defiance, as he said, "I live," while setting his face toward death. His defiance spills over into our lives. Luther tells us that in this, Christ promises, "And if I live, you, too, shall live with Me. For I, in turn, will maul and destroy death in such a way that it will be defeated not only for Me but also for you who believe in Me. And you will live as long as I do."[155]

Christ "tore the devil's belly and hell's jaws asunder"[156] for us, and we in turn will do the same. The particular form that death might take—fire, water, disease—doesn't especially matter. Death in all of its forms was defeated, and as Christ ripped through death, so will all who trust in him. Luther offered this challenge to Satan: "Therefore devour us if you can, or hurl us into the jaws of death, you will soon see and feel what you have done. We, in turn, will cause such a great disturbance in your belly and make an egress through your ribs that you wish you had rather devoured a tower, yes, an entire forest."[157]

Saint Paul mocked death in his letter to the Corinthians, "Where, O death, is your victory? Where, O death, is your sting?" (1 Corinthians 15:55). There Paul is repeating the taunting prophecy of Hosea 13:14, "Where, O death, are your plagues? Where, O grave, is your destruction?" More than once Luther picked up the same theme of ridicule. In an Easter sermon he said, "O death, where are thy teeth? Come, bite off one of my fingers. Thou formerly hadst a spear; what has become of it now? Christ has taken it from thee."[158] In another challenge, Luther dared death to do more than just bite. Commenting on Saint Paul's challenge, Luther wrote, "That is really snapping one's fingers at death and hell and saying: 'Dear death, do not bite me, but show your anger with me and kill me. I defy death and hell and challenge them to touch a hair on my head!'"[159] This sort of defiance is possible because death, hell, the Law, and Satan have been defeated, swallowed up in victory in Christ's resurrection. With victory assured, Luther happily pro-

vided the enemies' predicted response to defeat and ridicule,
"'I have lost,' they cry out, all together."[160]

The devil and death with all of their tricks and traps have
been overcome. But in difficult times, when the joy of Easter
wears thin, doubts move in to overwhelm joyful defiance. The
enemies return in full force. As courage fades, we are still
painfully aware of our sins and all the more so when facing
death. Satan uses guilt and despair to turn our attention
inward, away from God's grace. Luther gave this counsel for
such times:

> If the devil approaches us and says, Look here, see how great
> your sin is; see too, how bitter, how terrible is the death you
> must suffer; then you must counter with, "Devil, don't you
> know the power of my Lord Jesus' suffering, death, and resur-
> rection? In him there is eternal righteousness and eternal life.
> His resurrection from the dead is mightier than my sin, death,
> and hell, greater than heaven and earth. My death and sin are
> minute drops, but my Lord Jesus' death and resurrection is a
> vast ocean."[161]

Sin cannot harm us, and even death is powerless in the face
of Christ's resurrection. In Luther's words, Jesus boasts that his
followers are not dead but "sleep so lightly that I am able to
awaken them with my little finger."[162] Death, the great enemy,
can do nothing more serious than put Christians to sleep, a
sleep from which they will awaken at Christ's call.

In Greek mythology, a person's life and death were ordered
by the three Fates. These three goddesses controlled a thread
determining an individual's life span. The first Fate, Clotho,
spun the thread, and Lachesis decided on the length of life's
thread. Finally, Atropos cut the thread to bring about the person's death. Our thread—Christ's resurrection—is vastly different. It cannot be cut or broken, and in life and at death, it wraps
us securely in the life of Christ. We are disguised by it, so the
accusing, death-dealing Law cannot find us. Luther offered this
defiance: "For I am no longer the man you are looking for; I am
no longer a child of man, but a child of God, for I am baptized in

His blood and on His victory, and I am vested with all His possessions."[163] It is true that our reason and senses tell us that we must die, and it appears that we really are subject to the destructive whims of fate. At such times we must remember that appearances are deceiving, but the promises of God are not. Luther wrote, "To be sure, I feel and see that I and all other men must rot in the ground; but the Word informs me differently, namely, that I shall rise in great glory and live eternally."[164]

Luther was not one to preach what he would not practice. His teachings concerning death and his confidence in Christ's resurrection were brought to life as he and his family faced illness and grief. In 1527, his second child, Elizabeth, was born, but the little girl died within her first year. Writing to a friend, Luther asked for prayers on his behalf as he dealt with the new experience of a parent's grief. He wrote, "I would never have believed that a father's heart could be so tender for his child."[165]

In 1530, Luther received word that his father, Hans, was seriously ill. The letter of comfort and encouragement that Luther wrote to his father was circulated among Luther's friends and included in early collections of his works, suggesting that the letter was held in high regard even at that time. Because of the notoriety of his "heretical" son, Hans Luther had at times been slandered and hated. Luther commented that such experiences are the marks that identify us with Jesus and his suffering so that we may also one day share his glory. Luther encouraged his father to be confident even in illness, because we have a helper, Jesus Christ, who has destroyed death and now waits in heaven for us. Christ our Savior is faithful and righteous and will not forsake us, nor would he even want to do so. Even if Hans' illness ended in death and separation in this earthly life, the certainty of faith promised a reunion in the life to come. Luther wrote to his father: "For the departure from this life is a smaller thing to God than if I moved from you in Mansfeld to here, or if you moved from me in Wittenberg to Mansfeld. This is certainly true; it is only a matter of an hour's sleep, and all will be different."[166] There is no rest from the sin and wickedness of this life, Luther said, until we finally sleep in Christ, waiting for the day when he comes again to waken us. With trust in the Savior, Luther said to Hans, "Herewith I commend you to Him who loves you more than you love yourself."[167] Hans Luther fell asleep in Christ on May 29, 1530.

The following year Luther wrote a letter of comfort to his mother upon learning that she also was ill. Some of his opening comments may have seemed a little less than comforting, describing her illness as "a quite small chastisement in comparison with that which he inflicts upon the godless, and sometimes even his own dear children, when one person is beheaded, another burned, a third drowned, and so on."[168] Instead of regarding her illness with distress, Luther counseled his mother to accept her situation with thanksgiving, regarding it as slight suffering in comparison with the sufferings experienced by God's own Son.

As in the letter to his father, Luther directed his mother's attention to the risen and triumphant Christ. She would be able to find all needed comfort with the Savior who had overpowered sin and death on her behalf. We cannot overcome sin, death, and the devil by our own works, he wrote, but only by clinging in faith to Christ. As always, Luther advised defiance and encouraged his mother to confront the terrifying lies of death and the devil with firm trust in Christ, her true hero. Rendered powerless by Jesus' death and resurrection, death is only a shadow, a picture that frightens but can do no harm. In his letter, Luther confronted death as such: "Like a wooden image of death, you can terrify and challenge, but you have no power to strangle. For your victory, sting, and power have been swallowed up in Christ's victory. You can show your teeth, but you cannot devour, for God has given us the victory over you through Christ Jesus our Lord, to whom be praise and thanks."[169] Luther's mother passed safely through death into eternal life on June 30, 1531.

In his writings, Luther often expressed the love and happiness he found in his children. But in 1542, he again experienced a parent's grief when his 14-year-old daughter, Magdalena, died. He marveled at the sorrow that could exist side by side with the joy and hope of eternal life. Addressing his child, sleeping now in Christ, he said, "Poor, dear little Magdalena, there you are, peace be with you. Dear child, you will rise again, you will shine like a star, yes, like the sun. . . . I am joyful in spirit, but oh, how sad in the flesh. It is marvelous that I should know that she is certainly at rest, that she is well, and yet that I should be so sad."[170] Luther felt a sense of outrage against death for taking his beloved daughter, and he looked forward to the ultimate destruction of the devil and death, the enemies of life. He wrote to a friend, "I loved her dearly; but I dare say death will find its punishment on that Day together with him who is its author."[171]

As the end of Luther's life approached, he faced the last enemy with the same courage and confidence he had advised for others. His friend Justas Jonas reported that Luther prepared for death for an entire year. The reformer wrote verses from the psalms in a prayer book he carried. In his last days, his conversations were often filled with thoughts on death and eternity. Jonas reported that Luther stood at his window and prayed fervently out loud every day in the weeks before his death but was always happy and encouraged after his prayers.

In December 1545, Luther traveled to Mansfeld to mediate an argument between the brother counts Albert and Gebhard. When the dispute continued, Luther traveled again to Eisleben in January 1546 to offer his help. He often wrote back to his wife, Katie, describing his health and adventures. He wrote of a dangerous river crossing, calling the river "a great lady of the Anabaptist persuasion," covering the land "with waves of water and blocks of ice and threatening to baptize us."[172]

In February of the same year, he wrote to Katie again, complaining that her worrying had almost killed him several times, through a fire at the inn and by a falling stone that nearly crushed his head. He gave her credit for the calamities: "For this I thank your anxiety, but the dear angels protected me. I fear that unless you stop worrying the earth will swallow me up or the elements will persecute me."[173] He encouraged her to turn, instead, to one who was a better worrier on his behalf, Christ the Savior.

After advising Katie and so many others to trust in the promises of Christ, especially in the hour of death, he followed his own advice. In a note written in his Bible just ten days before his death, he commented on Jesus' words in John 8:51: "I tell you the truth, if anyone keeps my word, he will never see death." Luther's note read, "'Never see death.' How incredible these words are and how contradictory to public and daily experience! And yet it is true. If a man earnestly ponders God's Word in his heart, believes it, and falls asleep or dies over it, he sinks away and journeys forth before he is aware of death; he has surely departed blissfully in the Word thus believed and considered."[174]

In his last letter, dated February 14, 1546, Luther reported that the Mansfeld counts were reconciled in all but two or three points and he planned to meet with them to finish the agreement. A treaty was made between the brothers on February 16 and signed by Luther on February 17. During that day he felt faint and experienced pressure in his chest, feelings of illness that continued into the night. He died in the early morning hours of February 18, 1546. Reportedly, his last words confessed the hope and assurance he encouraged in others: "O heavenly Father, if I leave this body and depart I am certain that I will be with thee for ever and can never, never tear myself out of thy hands. 'God so loved the world that he gave his only begotten son, that whosoever believeth in him should not perish but have everlasting life.' Father, into thy hands I commend my spirit. Thou hast redeemed me, thou true God."[175]

Funeral services were held in Eisleben, but Luther was buried in Wittenberg, near his pulpit in the Castle Church. The official report of the burial referred to the promise of 1 Corinthians 15:43, stating that Luther's remains were "sown in dishonor in order to be raised on that day in eternal glory."[176]

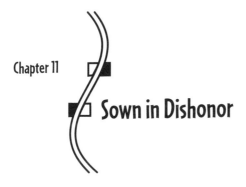

Chapter 11

Sown in Dishonor

In spite of every assurance and promise of the resurrection to come, even the strongest saints may still be easily shaken in faith when faced with the purely human fear of burial, of a body "sown in dishonor." In his writings, Luther provided new insight and new perspectives on that common practice and equally common fear.

Luther's remarks on Christian burial are centered on the hope of our resurrection to life on the Last Day. Luther insisted that we must learn a new vocabulary to properly discuss an uncomfortable topic. We must, he said, "learn to scrape our tongue and clear our eyes to enable us to view this in the light of God's Word and speak about it."[177] In this new language and understanding, those who die in Christ are not considered as the "dead" but as seed sown for the coming harvest. The apparent finality of death is in reality a promise of life to come. Luther pointed out that the early Christians called their burial places *coemeteria*, or sleeping chambers, a term that Luther favored over churchyards. Those who rest in sleeping chambers lie down in the knowledge that they will be awakened again at the proper time. Sleeping quarters and harvest fields are places of future activity. Luther commented that "the cemetery or burial ground does not indicate a heap of the dead, but a field full of kernels, known as God's kernels, which will verdantly blossom forth again and grow more beautifully than can be imagined."[178]

God surrounds us with daily lessons in our new vocabulary of death and life. It is hard to believe that a body, buried and decayed, can possibly be raised to life again, so God graciously illustrates the process for us. Saint Paul explained in 1 Corinthians 15:36, "What you sow does not come to life unless it dies." A seed is buried and decays, sprouting a root and stem, and finally an ear of grain filled with new kernels. Luther exclaimed, "What a precious artist Saint Paul becomes here, painting and carving the resurrection into everything that grows on earth!"[179] If we had never before seen trees blossom or bear fruit, Luther said, we would think such things were miracles. If God can accomplish such a miracle with a small seed, then he will certainly create a glorious new life for his people. "In short," Luther wrote, "we have as many living proofs of the resurrection as we behold kernels and seeds sprouting in the field or in the garden. And so we say: 'Life is emerging from death everywhere.'"[180]

A farmer, of course, is accustomed to the miracle of new life. He sows seeds in the ground, confidently waiting for the harvest to come. Just as the body is "sown in dishonor" only to be "raised in glory," the buried seeds decay to nothing in order to grow into the grain of the summer harvest. We become doubtful when we see the helpless and apparently hopeless condition of the body to be buried. How can it possibly come to life again? When sown in the ground, the kernels of wheat or other grain display the same helpless condition; they cannot move or free themselves. Once again, this small miracle of creation illustrates the truth of God's promises. Luther was amazed that a sprout from a tiny, weak seed could force its way up through ground so dry and hard that the farmer can barely work it with his tools. Yet with the power implanted by God, a helpless seed forces its way through hard ground and gravel until it reaches the light. There is a lesson here to calm our fears, as Luther explained, "In view of this, should God not be able to do that with us, in accordance with His Word, that we come forth with a new strength when He wants to raise us up?"[181]

God does not allow us to be buried in the ground with the intent that we should remain there any more than a farmer plants seeds in order to forget about them. Death is necessary, Luther said, and bluntly insisted on God's desire that each believer "lie down and decompose"[182] in order to receive from God's creating hand a new and beautiful form. In fact, Luther said, it is only when they are removed from sight, decayed to dust, and forgotten and dismissed by the world as beyond hope that the dead really begin to live. They then "become a precious treasure which God himself holds dear and precious and glories in beyond all else. And the more they are forgotten in the eyes of the world the more he honors and glorifies them."[183]

However dignified and proper a funeral might be, a burial is still a burial. Luther was aware of that undignified reality and said, "Moreover, the shame of our being buried so nastily is covered with a dignity which is called the resurrection of Jesus Christ, by which it is so adorned that the sun is put to shame when it looks upon it and the beloved angels cannot gaze upon it sufficiently."[184]

If we focus on the fact of the burial, on the decaying, corrupted body, faith may well fail us. Instead, we must again turn our attention to the promises of God's Word and the examples of life from death that God has provided. Trees that appear dead blossom into life in the spring. Seeds "tossed aside" by a farmer grow into a summer field ripe for harvest. In the same way, Luther said, the bodies that God has consigned to burial and decay in the "winter" of death will be raised and glorified in the "summer" of judgment day. Saint Paul spoke with certainty about the harvest, Luther said, so that we will not keep our attention on death or disease but on the beautiful harvest to come. Luther explained Paul's efforts to focus our thoughts in the right direction:

[The body] is buried and sown as something perishable and it will rise up imperishable. It is sown in weakness and will rise in power. It is sown a natural body and will rise a spiritual body, etc. Thus he is constantly turning our hearts, because he cannot turn our eyes, away from that which the eyes see to that which God is saying and to Christ, so that we may have no doubt that he will bring us with Christ. So anyone who can believe this will have good comfort in his own death and the death of other people.[185]

The language of faith and our new, heavenly vocabulary tell us that bodies sown in dishonor will some day be raised in glory. "Seeds" sown in weakness will be raised in power in the harvest of God's eternal summer.

Chapter 12

Like the Sleep of an Infant

Countless children have delivered their souls' safekeeping into God's hands in a common bedtime prayer:

Now I lay me down to sleep;
I pray the Lord my soul to keep.
If I should die before I wake,
I pray the Lord my soul to take.

Believers know that at death their souls will certainly be safe in the Lord's care. But the question remains, just where are those souls? What are they doing and what is their condition? Does the soul "sleep" and "rest," or is it wakeful and enjoying Christ's presence?

The condition of the soul between temporal death and the resurrection on the Last Day is addressed in Scripture in different ways. God's Word speaks of death as a sleep (1 Thessalonians 4:14: "God will bring with Jesus those who have fallen asleep in him.") but also indicates that after death the saints are found immediately in Christ's presence (Luke 23:43: "Today you will be with me in paradise."). Luther was comfortable with the mystery of the soul's condition, viewing the question as something that lies outside of our severely limited understanding of time and eternity. He speculated about the place and activity of the soul after death and did not hesitate to give his opinions. But he also had enough confidence—much like the faith expressed in the child's bedtime prayer—to let the

Lord worry about keeping the souls of believers safe. Luther's acceptance of the mystery is evident in his expression of what appear to be conflicting views on the subject. At times he wrote of the soul's immediate peace and rest in Christ's presence, yet he also spoke of the soul resting in sleep until being awakened on the Last Day. Luther was content to let God resolve what seems to be yet another contradiction in terms. Speaking on Isaiah 57:2: "Those who walk uprightly enter into peace; they find rest as they lie in death," Luther said, "But how the saints sleep is not for us to know. It is enough for us to know that they are reclining in God's repose, sleeping and resting in a life that has been made peaceful. How they experience repose and sleep is beyond our understanding."[186]

The Old Testament references to the Lord as the God of Abraham indicated to Luther that the patriarchs, even after death, were alive and active in God's service. Commenting on Genesis 26:24: "I am the God of your father Abraham," Luther said that Abraham, even in death, was living and serving God. "But," Luther wrote, "what sort of life that may be, whether he is asleep or awake, is another question. How the soul is resting we are not to know, but it is certain that it is living."[187]

Luther was also content to let the location of the soul after death remain a mystery. Ecclesiastes 9:10 states, "Whatever your hand finds to do, do it with all your might, for in the grave, where you are going, there is neither working nor planning nor knowledge nor wisdom." Commenting on that passage, Luther said that this place of souls, or "grave," exists outside this world, but he admitted that we do not know exactly where or what it might be. But we are not required to know or understand these things. It is enough, in Luther's thought, to know that God has matters well in hand. If we commit ourselves to the Lord's safekeeping in earthly sleep, then we should with all confidence commit ourselves, body and soul, to Christ in the sleep of death.

Part of our inability to resolve the issue of the soul's condition lies in our attempts to sharply define death and sleep in the familiar terms of our present life. Trying to explain the situation in the light of God's Word, Luther described a sort of wakeful, living sleep. A mother watching her peacefully sleeping infant does not exclaim in alarm that the child is dead. We may say in a figure of speech that a man taking a nap is "dead to the world," but we know that he is very much alive while he sleeps. Luther uses these images to explain the sleep of the soul:

> God looks upon the death of all men like the sleep of an infant slumbering at rest in its cradle. It is not eating, then, or drinking, and doing things like a living person, but sleeping like a log, dead to the world, except for the sound of its breathing. Of course, the mother does not think of the child as dead, but alive. Now someone who's alive is supposed to eat, drink, stand, walk, and be active in the way a living person ordinarily is. We must not confuse the issue. For although a man who is asleep is not busy with things like a person who is alive, yet we do not say, This man is dead, but alive, even though all his activity as a living person has ceased. Now, in the selfsame way, as we think of those who slumber, God speaks about those who have died. He says, To me those lying in the grave are not dead; to you humans they are, of course, but in my own time I shall awaken and raise them from the dead.[188]

In Luther's thought, the soul, in some unknown way, is active in the sleep of death. So while Luther could describe death as a deep, dreamless sleep, he could at the same time speak of the soul experiencing visions and hearing God and the angels. Commenting on the prophetic vision of Abraham as described in Genesis chapter 15, Luther repeated a story by Saint Augustine. A certain physician who doubted the doctrines of the resurrection and the soul's immortality fell asleep and dreamed of a visit from a young man. The visitor called the sleeping doctor by name, and when the doctor admitted to seeing and hearing him, the young man asked how it was that he could see with his eyes closed. How could he hear if he was asleep? Taking this account in hand, Luther said, "Therefore learn and believe that there are other spiritual eyes with which those who believe in Christ see when the eyes of the body have been closed by death or have rather been entirely destroyed."[189]

A man wrapped in ordinary sleep may be unaware of all sorts of activity going on around him. As opposed to that purely human slumber, the soul in its wakeful sleep of death is quite busy. Speaking of Abraham's death as recorded in Genesis chapter 25, Luther said that the departed soul does not sleep in a state of unawareness; "it is, more properly speaking, awake and has visions and conversations with the angels and God. Therefore the sleep of the future life is deeper than that of this life, and yet the soul lives before God."[190]

Our temporal definitions of *death* and *sleep* make it difficult to understand these things, and our captivity to earthly time does not help the situation. In this world, time is a consecutive thing, one event happening after another in proper order. God's "divine computation of time"[191] is another matter entirely. Preaching on the raising of Jairus' daughter, Luther advised his congregation against attempts at calculating the number of years between death and life, between burial and the resurrection. God's timing is very different: "For he does not calculate by tens, hundreds, or thousands of years, nor measure the years consecutively, the one preceding, the other following, as we must do in this life; but he grasps everything in a moment, the beginning, middle, and end of the whole human race and of all time."[192] In another attempt to explain God's timing, Luther used an illustration from everyday life. Preaching on 1 Peter chapter 3 and Christ's descent into hell, Luther said:

> Let me give an illustration. If a piece of wood is lying some distance away from you, or if you are looking at it lengthwise, then you cannot examine it well, but if it is lying close to you, or if you are standing on top of it and can look at it crosswise, then you have a full view of it. Thus we on earth cannot understand this life; for it is always moving along consecutively, step by step until the Last Day.[193]

God does not need to see things happen step by step. For him, Luther said, everything takes place in a moment, and "for Him the first human being is just as close as the human being who is to be born last. And He sees everything at one time, just as the human eye can bring together in one moment two things that are far from each other."[194]

We can see objects near and far in one glance, but we cannot so easily reconcile past, present, and future events into one image. Theologian Paul Althaus gave this possible explanation of the relationship of time and eternity: "Because our periods of time are no longer valid in God's eternity, the Last Day surrounds our life as an ocean surrounds an island. Wherever we reach the boundaries of this life . . . everywhere the Last Day dawns in the great contemporaneity of eternity."[195] Luther also spoke of the immediate dawn of eternal life. He tried to take note of the exact moment in which he fell asleep or woke up but was never able to catch the time or prevent himself from falling asleep before he was aware of it. He commented that death and resurrection would be like that: "We pass away, and on Judgment Day we return before we are aware of it, nor shall we know how long we have been dead."[196]

When the unknown moment of the Last Day arrives, Christ, the firstfruits of the resurrection life, will call believers from their graves. The deep, watchful sleep of death will be done. Many times during his earthly ministry, Jesus summoned the dead to life. To the young man of Nain in his funeral procession, Christ said, "Young man, I say to you, get up!" (Luke 7:14). He called to his friend, "Lazarus, come out!" (John 11:43) and to Jairus' daughter, "Little girl, I say to you, get up!" (Mark 5:41).Those who slept in death were awakened by the Savior's call. On the Last Day, Christ will again call out his command and we—though sleeping deeply in death—will instantly hear and respond. The deep and dreamless sleep of death is a light sleep after all. Luther commented, "It is true, we sleep much more soundly in bed than we do in the churchyard!"[197] Although he expected to be asleep in death on that day, Luther said that his sleep would be "so sweet and light that the Lord scarcely need open his mouth before I hear him and rise to eternal life."[198] Again Luther explained that he expected to rest in watchful sleep until Christ was to come and knock on his grave, calling, "Arise, arise, Martin Luther, come forth! Then in a moment we shall rise, as if from a light, pleasant sleep, and live forever with the Lord, rejoicing."[199] In 1 Thessalonians 5:9,10, Saint Paul wrote, "For God did not appoint us to suffer wrath but to receive salvation through our Lord Jesus Christ. He died for us so that, whether we are awake or asleep, we may live together with him." Actively awake in love and service, taking rest in earthly sleep, or watchful in the sleep of death, we are alert for Christ's call to life on the day of resurrection. The timing of that great event—and our souls' safekeeping—rest in his hands.

Chapter 13

Raised in Glory

If people of Luther's day looked for immortality, they sought it through the church, in the sacraments, in the merits of the saints, or in their own works. Today scientific research offers what at least some people hope will prove to be a path to eternal life—cloning. Controversy and popular interest surround the subject. Some couples hope that cloning might allow them to have children when other methods have failed. To others the promise of cloning appears to offer a kind of immortality for themselves, for family members, or even pets. One man gave this motive for his interest: "I can thumb my nose at Mr. Death and say, 'You might get me, but you're not going to get all of me.' . . . The special formula that is me will live on into another lifetime. It's a partial triumph over death."[200] Ethicist Arthur Caplan of the University of Pennsylvania was not as confident. He said that cloning "can't make you immortal because clearly the clone is a different person. If I take twins and shoot one of them, it will be faint consolation to the dead one that the other one is still running around, even though they are genetically identical. So the road to immortality is not through cloning."[201]

Indeed, cloning is no more useful in achieving eternal life than an attempt to earn God's favor with our own merit. Martin Luther pointed down the one road to immortality, a road leading to the cross and the empty tomb of Jesus Christ. It is a road we have already traveled in Holy Baptism. Because of that we have much more than just the hope of immortality. To Luther's way of thinking, the resurrection is already two thirds accomplished in us. We will be finally and completely clothed in immortality when Christ returns on the Last Day and summons us from our light and wakeful sleep. Luther considered the resurrection of the body as secondary in importance to this first, spiritual resurrection. He wrote that our hearts, or consciences, and souls "have already passed through death and grave and are in heaven with Christ, dwell there and rejoice over it. And in that way we have the two best parts, much more than half, of the resurrection behind us. And because Christ animates and renews the heart by faith, He will surely drag the decomposed rascal after Him and clothe him again, so that we can behold Him and live with Him. For that is His Word and work on which we are baptized and live and die."[202]

There was no doubt for Luther that our bodies—"the decomposed rascals"—will be raised to life on the Last Day. Christ, our head, was raised, and where the head is, the members of his body must follow. It is a natural process, Luther pointed out, much like the birth of men and animals—the head emerges first and the body follows. Christ, the firstfruits, the "firstborn from among the dead" (Colossians 1:18), was raised for our sake. Luther said, "For as by his resurrection he has taken everything with himself, so that heaven and earth, sun and moon, and all creatures must both rise and become new, so he will also take us along."[203]

Luther had advised believers to contemplate the wounds of Christ to remember his suffering and death. But there will be another opportunity to see those wounds. Luther felt that the Lord of life will, on the Last Day, display those same glorious scars to the world. The events of that day will happen quickly, Luther said, as everything on earth is consumed in a moment, and we are changed in order to live with Christ forever. The summons to life will also happen in God's own timing, in that brief, eternal moment. Luther noted that God "will do the same thing with Christians that he did with Christ, whom he raised up from the locked and sealed grave in the twinkling of an eye, so that in the selfsame moment he was in it and out of it."[204] He rose, Luther said, "like a lightning flash from heaven"[205] and will raise the members of his body from the dust of the earth, from watery graves, or wherever they rest. Lightly sleeping, they will hear the call of Christ and come forth to "stand in full view, utterly pure and clean as the bright sun."[206]

The call and command to life will be in Christ's own voice, Luther said, speculating that perhaps it could be in Hebrew. But even if the call is in no one particular language, it will be a shout to wake the dead. On the Last Day, God will extend his great power over us and with one word, one command, will raise all people from the dead and grant eternal life to believers. Just as Christ spoke a word of command to Lazarus, to Jairus' daughter, to the widow's son, restoring them to life, in the same way he will tell us to rise. Luther rejoiced, "That one word is so powerful that death must yield, and life again returns."[207]

Although we already have more than half of the resurrection realized within ourselves, the "decomposed rascal" that is this body of flesh must be changed. What was "sown in dishonor" waits for Christ's summons to be "raised in glory." Luther took great delight in describing the new, spiritual bodies that we will receive on the Last Day. There was no question in his mind that it would be done—since God created the first man from the dust of the earth, he can as easily create a spiritual body from this present body. There is no way that our limited understanding can compare this body of flesh with the body we will have on the Last Day. What comparison is there, Luther asked, between a clod of dirt and a living, breathing human body? He pointed out that the kings of the Old Testament, and even Christ himself, were called David's seed or Abraham's seed. How different, Luther said, is the seed—he calls it a drop of blood or the beginning of man— from the great kings or even the King of kings? Again, no comparison is possible.

The new resurrection body, Luther wrote, will be light and agile and will soar effortlessly like a spark or like the sun in the sky. In words that sound something like the trademark description of a comic book superhero, Luther told his congregation

that the new body "will be so strong that with one finger it will
be able to carry this church, with one toe it will be able to move
a tower and play with a mountain as children play with a ball.
And in the twinkling of an eye it will be able to leap to the
clouds or traverse a hundred miles."[208] With our transformed
bodies we will be able to see or hear things one hundred miles
away, see through walls, or be in heaven or on earth in a
moment. We will, Luther assured us, be brighter and more
beautiful than the sun or moon. The finest garments and gold
of kings will be "sheer dirt in comparison with us."[209]

With these new spiritual bodies, we will have no need to eat
or drink. We will have God and be with God. Luther wrote that
God "has sufficient of everything forever in Himself, for He
lives in and through Himself."[210] As God has everything, we
also will have everything we need in and through him. On the
Last Day, Christ, who reigns now through Word and sacrament, will turn the kingdom over to his Father so that "God
may be all in all" (1 Corinthians 15:28). There will be no more
need for earthly things, for food, family, governors, or princes.
There will be no need to establish a home or raise children,
although Luther commented that men and women will retain
their distinctive natures: "Everybody will remain what he was
created, whether man or woman. For Scripture says that God
created male and female. He will not change His creation."[211]
On the Last Day, Luther said, "Only One will remain; He will
be called God. He Himself will be Preacher, Comforter, Father,
Mother, Lord, and Emperor. . . . Nothing will be needed
beyond having Him."[212]

Simply the sight of God will give us more joy and delight
than any creature of earth could give. No one, Luther said, will
be able to terrify or confuse us again. On that day, it will be the
work of the Holy Spirit to "instantly perfect our holiness."[213]
Faith will be replaced by glory and our limited understanding
will give way to new knowledge. Luther wrote, "There will be
a true and perfect knowledge of God, a right reason, and a
good will, neither moral nor theological but heavenly, divine,
and eternal."[214]

Commenting on Saint Paul's words that "star differs from star in splendor" (1 Corinthians 15:41), Luther spoke of degrees of glory in the resurrection life. "For instance," he wrote, "Peter's and Paul's will be the glory of apostles; one person will partake of the glory of a martyr, another of that of a pious bishop or preacher; each one in accord with the works which he has performed. . . . And yet with regard to person they are alike and they have the same essence, and all will have equal joy and bliss in God."[215] Everyone will have the same heavenly "essence," sharing as members of Christ the nature of spiritual flesh and blood that defines our risen head.

The corruptible rascal of a body, shunned and buried as quickly as possible—even the body of a prince or king—will be transformed at the resurrection into a glorified and honorable form. Luther described the joyful reaction of creation and Creator to the newly risen body: "Every creature will be amazed over it, all the angels will sing praises and smile admiringly at it, and God himself will take delight in it."[216]

In the Nicene Creed, we confess that we "look for the resurrection of the dead and the life of the world to come." In keeping with that future-directed sight, Luther advised us to start thinking now about the resurrection life that will begin on the Last Day. Then we will realize that we need not cling to this temporal life. The illustration of a needlepoint picture or tapestry is sometimes used to compare this temporal life with the life of the world to come. In this life we see only the back of the picture, which is not much of a picture at all, with all of its knots and loose, dangling threads. On the day of resurrection, we will recognize the completed tapestry of life, seeing it as God has always seen it. On that day, we will have all that we need, and what we need will be found in God. Luther wrote, "In short, whatever delights your heart shall be yours abundantly. For we read that God Himself will be everything to everyone. But wherever God is, all good things that one may wish for must also be present."[217] On that day, we will finally see with eyes of spiritual flesh what we before could only see with eyes of faith.

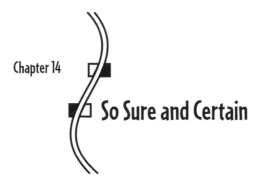

Chapter 14

So Sure and Certain

Filled with uncertainty in the face of death, a cancer patient expressed her fear as well as her wish for a place in which to anchor hope, "Many days bring stark terror. . . . I sometimes wish that I had a belief system."[218] Author Daniel Callahan expresses a similar uncertainty and a faint sort of hope: "Can death, and the life in which it is embedded, be transcended? I do not see this for myself, but I hope to live the remainder of my days in a way that at least puts me in a position to be (as Wordsworth put it) 'surprised by joy.' It is unlikely, but perhaps not impossible. I wait and watch."[219]

Such uncertainty is common, although we might imagine that at least Christ's disciples felt the certain hope of the resurrection. For three years they walked with Jesus, listened to his teachings, and witnessed his miracles. But when he died, any hope they may have had died with him. Luther wrote of their despair: "When He died and was buried, there was no perception or expectation of life. And it was so very hard for the disciples to believe that the Christ lying in the grave behind a sealed rock was the Lord over death and grave. They themselves said (Luke 24:21): 'We had hoped that he was the one to redeem Israel.'"[220] A world of lost hope is evident in those few words, "We had hoped that he was the one. . . ."

The despairing disciples trusted the evidence of their senses and the logical, though limited, arguments of reason. They walked with Jesus and witnessed his power. But they also witnessed his humiliating death. They saw his body hanging on the cross and lying in the grave. All hope of life and victory stopped short at the sealed tomb. Without the resurrection they could not understand the cross, and for them the salvation of Israel apparently ended in a grave.

For us, as for the disciples, the thread of the resurrection becomes nearly invisible at times, overwhelmed by the evidence of our reason and senses. Only faith, granted through the power of the Holy Spirit, magnifies the presence of that thread and makes it visible again. With faith comes the certain knowledge that Christ was raised from death, defeating death for us. We know that bodies sown in dishonor will be raised in glory, that bodies resting in watchful sleep will be awakened to new and glorious life.

Faith enables us to be more certain of what we cannot see than of what we can see, however illogical that may be. At the funeral service of Elector John, Luther told his congregation that they could be more sure of the fact that their prince would one day rise from death than of the fact that his body lay there in front of their eyes. Examples of that sort of faith and assurance are all around us, if we care to look for them. We might grow tired of a long, cold winter, but if we stop to think about it, no one really doubts that spring and summer will shortly follow. God gave us the change of seasons, Luther said, to serve as a symbol that he will bring our transformed bodies out of death into life.

Luther used ordinary pictures from daily life, of farmers, seeds, and the harvest, to illustrate the certainty of the coming resurrection. Farmers sow seeds in firm confidence that their work will result in a harvest. They are so sure of the harvest that they are willing to part with the grain or seed they already have, secure in the knowledge that it will produce an as yet unseen crop. Luther described the farmer's faith: "He is so sure and certain of the growth of the grain as though he already beheld it before him. Indeed, he is much surer of this than of what he here has in hand. Otherwise he would not be so foolish as to throw it away for no reason at all."[221]

It is one thing, however, to talk with assurance about seeds and crops and quite another to think and speak with hope in front of an open grave or at a hospital bedside. If we take the seed's point of view as opposed to the farmer's, we find a more familiar opinion. If the seed, Luther said, "could see and feel what is happening to it, it would be constrained to think that it is lost forever."[222] The seed is under the impression that the farmer no longer wants it, that it is being thrown out for good. The farmer has a different story to tell. He would explain to the frightened seed its role in the coming harvest, describing its future as a beautiful, growing stalk of grain.

In much the same way, Luther said, God casts handfuls of his "seeds," his Christians, into the cemetery, putting them into the ground. This burial looks like the end, but God entertains different thoughts. He allows the burial "in order that His little kernels might emerge again most beautifully during the pleasant coming summer following this miserable existence. He is as sure of this as though it had already come to pass and had been carried out."[223]

Such assurance is possible for us only because its foundation is found outside of ourselves and our own efforts. How can a buried body possibly rise to life again? It is not only possible, it is an absolute certainty, because this certainty is based in Jesus Christ. Considering a funeral procession, Luther expressed astonishment that he and the corpse could one day rise to life together, but he also described the source of his confidence: "How so, or by what power? Not by myself or by virtue of any merit on earth, but by this one Christ. And that is indeed certain, far more certain than the fact that I will be buried and see someone else buried, which I know with certainty and behold with my eyes."[224] The coming harvest is more real to the farmer than the seed he holds in his hand; for the sake of that harvest he is willing to risk the seed. The day of resurrection is to be more real for us than the fact of our own death and burial; for the sake of that day, God allows his "seeds," his people, to be buried in hope. Luther said, "A florin in a purse or pocket is a genuine florin and also remains genuine when I take it out and hold it in my hand. The only difference is that it is no longer concealed."[225] The treasure of our eternal life is hidden for now in Christ, but it is no less real on this day than it will be on the day of his return.

The hope and assurance of eternal life are grounded entirely in the promises of God. If God were to follow our plans, Luther said, there would be no honor in that for him. God does not let the evidence of our senses govern his actions. "On the contrary," Luther wrote, "His concern is to make His words come true: 'Death, I will be your death' (Hosea 13:14), 'I will devour you and will revive him whom you devoured, or I will no longer be God.'"[226]

We should not be surprised at what appears to be an unusual progression of events—that suffering, death, and burial should lead to life. It is very much in keeping with God's character that he should act in this way. Luther pointed out that God makes everything out of nothing and makes nothing out of everything. In the Genesis account, God reduced Joseph to nothing, to slavery and imprisonment. "And when it seemed that Joseph was ruined and lost," Luther said, "He makes everything out of him, that is, the greatest man in the world."[227] All appearances to the contrary, when man is "lying under the ground, stinking like a rotting carcass, and consumed by maggots and worms,"[228] there is found the seed of resurrection. Luther remarked, "But if it is true that God cannot lie or deny or abandon his deity, this article [of the resurrection], too, must become true."[229]

Believing that a buried corpse will live forever, believing that we are still children of God when we feel our own sin and guilt—these things, Luther said, require a divine wisdom that is not governed by human perception. Faith in the Word of God provides the necessary proof. Luther wrote that by the power of Christ's resurrection, "he proved that Scripture is more than the feeling, the thinking, and the experiencing of all men."[230] Faith gives us greater insight than our eyes or senses can provide. By faith we know that our resurrection life has already begun, even though it is hidden for now, like coins in a pocket. The treasure is there, but as yet unseen.

Worldly wisdom generally claims that something must be seen to be believed. Faith tells us that things must be believed in order to be seen. Luther described faith's unusual perception of eternal life in his typically graphic and gruesome terms:

> To be destroyed, to be buried in the ground, to be consumed and reduced to dust, and indeed with such foulness that, as cadavers are commonly depicted, owls are born from the human brain and serpents from the intestines—this is not what it means to have eternal life, is it? Yet here faith must come to a firm conclusion and expect resurrection and a return to life. So great and wonderful an art it is to believe and hope![231]

Luther expected skeptics to question such unusual confidence. If there were any basis to the message of the resurrection, they say, then experience would provide some useful evidence for it. But human experience cannot reconcile the opposing facts—we have defeated death, yet we are still subject to death. Luther replied that we "must first believe contrary to our experience what cannot be believed humanly, and that we must feel what we do not feel."[232]

The Old Testament patriarch Jacob provided Luther with an example of the power of faith over feeling. In Genesis 48:21, Jacob told his son Joseph, "I am about to die, but God will be with you and take you back to the land of your fathers." Jacob was so sure that God would take his people back to Israel, it was as though he could see it happening. That, Luther said, is the power of faith. In the world's eyes, faith appears to be a feeble thing, but it is not. In its very weakness, it can accomplish more than all human feeling. Luther described faith as "so active and so mighty that it tears heaven and earth apart and opens all graves in the twinkling of an eye. And if you but remain with it, you shall live eternally by it and become lord over all things, even though your faith is feeble and your feeling strong."[233]

The strength of feeble faith comes about only through the power of the Holy Spirit. Faith can make decisions contrary to human reason and submit to the Word, Luther said, when the

Spirit is at work in men's hearts. Luther found the Spirit at work in the Genesis story of Joseph and Jacob in Egypt. Joseph did not hesitate to honor his father, Jacob, a shepherd, even though the Egyptian people despised shepherds. The decision to disregard the might and culture of a powerful earthly kingdom required great courage and confidence in a kingdom yet to come. Such courage, Luther commented, "hopes for much greater things than the kingdom of Egypt or the whole earth, because it has faith and hope in the resurrection of the dead. . . . For it is a great thing to despise the kingdom of Egypt for the sake of a father who is a shepherd and brothers who sold him and are parricides. But such is the heart when the Holy Spirit comes."[234] The Spirit enables feeble faith to overpower strong feeling and leads us to firm trust in the promises of Christ.

Students in an art class were assigned the challenge of doing a realistic painting, a still life of a box containing small, specific objects—a playing card, a Christmas ornament, and so on. The finished paintings were displayed beside the still life boxes. One student achieved the desired result, producing a painting that did in fact look more "real" than the box beside it. The play of light and shadow in the painting made the painted objects appear more solid than the items in the still life. Faith that trusts in Jesus Christ is able to paint the same realistic picture of eternal life, a life more vivid and real than the life now lived. Our reason, our senses, and our experience show us only this present life and its "natural" and expected end of death. Luther expressed a different sight: "But the faith that clings to Christ is able to engender far different thoughts. It can envisage a new existence. It can form an image and gain sight of a condition where this perishable, wretched form is erased entirely and replaced by a pure and celestial essence."[235] The treasure of coins tucked in a pocket is still a treasure although it remains unseen. The coming harvest is more real to the farmer than the seeds of grain he tosses into the ground. With faith's vivid sight, Christians confess together, "I look for the resurrection of the dead and the life of the world to come."

Chapter 15

Woven by Christ's Victory

Saint Paul's lessons in resurrection hope were sparked by serious doubts and questions: "How can some of you say that there is no resurrection of the dead? . . . How are the dead raised? With what kind of body will they come?" Questions like that cannot be accurately answered with the world's knowledge. The answers lie in the wisdom of faith, answers understood from God's point of view and expressed in a new and heavenly vocabulary. In these matters, Luther said, we must "learn to distinguish between the world's eyes and God's eyes, between reason, according to which the old man remains in the grave, and faith, by which we are new, heavenly men and receive totally new hearts and thoughts about death and all misfortune."[236]

There will never be—in this life—a time when we completely "arrive," when we fully understand this new wisdom of faith. Paul hammered home the lessons of the resurrection with many arguments and examples. He knew it was a lesson we must never stop learning. Luther stressed the same point:

> In fact, the time never comes when we have preached and heard enough concerning the significance of Christ's resurrection. We are not preaching anything new, but always, without ceasing, about the man who is called Jesus Christ, true God and true man, who died for our sins and rose for our justification. Yet even if we were again and again to preach about and dwell upon these events, we could never really exhaust their meaning. We would

remain like infants and young children, just learning to speak, scarcely able to form half words, yes, scarcely quarter words.[237]

Luther followed his own advice. He spoke often on the resurrection of Christ, of its power and benefits, and of our own feeble faith and easy doubts. Like Saint Paul, he used visible examples from daily life to express invisible truths of faith. Seeds and sleeping chambers, farmers and florins filled his sermons and lectures about Christ's death and victory. The thread of the resurrection moved through Luther's thought, sometimes expressed directly, and other times mentioned only briefly, nearly invisible like the unseen hope it supplies. However invisible it might be, the thread cannot be pulled free without destroying the whole of faith in Christ. In discussing Paul's arguments, Luther gave this advice on the article of the resurrection:

> For ponder this yourself and see what a sin it is to entertain any doubt regarding this article, since Paul states that this is the same as denying God and Christ, as renouncing your faith, Baptism, and the Gospel, giving these the lie and saying: "I believe that there is no God, no Christ, and that all that is said about faith is an abominable lie."[238]

To deny that Christ rose from the dead is to deny Christ. There is no middle ground.

The resurrection and the hope of eternal life are not just matters of doctrine firmly held for the sake of Christendom in general. As ever with Luther, the emphasis remained—what Jesus Christ did, he did "for you." The thread of the resurrection secures the faith of the whole church and yet wraps itself around each individual believer in Baptism. That baptismal faith is nourished in the hope of the resurrection through the Lord's Supper and the preaching of the Word. It is a faith expressed in a life of dying and rising, dying to sin and rising daily to a life of love and service. It is a faith that enables us to face trouble and suffering with courage and confidence.

Above all else, the resurrection provides assurance in the face of death; it is the event that shapes the "defiant comfort" of

Christian hope. Luther expressed this singular confidence in an Easter Eve sermon:

> The words, Christ is risen from the dead, we should blazon and inscribe with letters so large that just one letter would be as large as a steeple, yes, as heaven and earth, so that we would see and hear, know and think of, nothing but this article. For we speak and confess this article in prayer, not just as an incident that has occurred, as we routinely tell some idle tale, or story or happening, but as something firmly set in our hearts, real and alive. And we call this faith, when we are so grounded on it and as firmly caught up in it as if nothing else were ever written, for Christ is risen.[239]

That is the confidence we have, the assurance that we will pass safely through death into eternal life, if we "wrap ourselves in the death of the Son of God and cover and veil ourselves with his resurrection."[240] Veiled in the resurrection we can squarely face the unknown, narrow passageway of death and the indignity of burial, knowing without doubt that we will rest in Christ's presence, sleeping lightly in anticipation of the summons to life on the Last Day.

In order to remain firm in faith, Luther advised us not to dwell on the frightening aspects of death, but to focus intently on the death and resurrection of Jesus Christ:

> If you gaze steadfastly at this mirror and image, at Christ the Lord, who died and rose again, you will see where you will go and where those will go who have not fallen asleep in Christ, namely, that God intends to bring with him you and all others who have been baptized and have fallen asleep in Christ, because he has wrapped them in Christ's death and included them in his resurrection and does not intend to leave them lying under the ground, even though for our reason and five senses there is no reason why this should be so, in order that faith may find room and we learn to trust God even in that which we do not see.[241]

On the Last Day, that which we have never seen will be visible. What was real by faith will be revealed to sight. Luther spoke of the present victory that will expand to still greater triumph:

> For although [death] is not yet entirely swallowed up in us, the victory gained by Christ is already present, and through Gospel, Baptism, and faith it has become our victory. On the Last Day, when we have taken off the old, terrestrial, perishable garment and put on a new celestial one, we can destroy [death] completely with this victory.[242]

On that great day, our thread of resurrection hope will weave itself into a finished robe of immortality.

Saint Paul described the dress of immortality that will be ours, writing in 1 Corinthians 15:53,54: "For the perishable must clothe itself with the imperishable, and the mortal with immortality. When the perishable has been clothed with the imperishable, and the mortal with immortality, then the saying that is written will come true: 'Death has been swallowed up in victory.'" Paul pulled those words, the promise of final victory, from the pages of the Old Testament. There the prophet Isaiah wrote of a covering woven from death instead of life, a garment of perishable flesh and empty hope destined for destruction: "On this mountain he will destroy the shroud that enfolds all peoples, the sheet that covers all nations; he will swallow up death forever" (Isaiah 25:7,8). On a mountain called Calvary, God used death to destroy death, and in a dark and empty tomb not too far from that mountain, death was swallowed up forever.

Saint Paul spoke of this present life and death, Luther said, as nothing more serious than an article of clothing that must be worn for now but will in time be discarded and replaced: "He makes no more of death and grave than he does of taking off an old torn garment and casting it away. To him the resurrection is like putting on a beautiful new garment called *immortalitas*, incorruptibility, or immortality. It is spun and woven by Christ's victory."[243] The frightening garment of death, the smothering shroud, will be discarded in favor of a garment created out of life and victory.

Saint Paul's teaching on resurrection hope began with questions. He ended his lesson with a few questions of his own, defiant, mocking questions thrown in the face of the last enemy: "Where, O death, is your victory? Where, O death, is your sting?" (1 Corinthians 15:55). Through his death and resurrection, Jesus Christ snatched the victory from death and dressed us in his own conquering might. He is the one in whom we find—with Saint Paul and with Luther—the answer to all of our questions: "Thanks be to God! He gives us the victory through our Lord Jesus Christ" (1 Corinthians 15:57).

Endnotes

[1]Martin Luther, *Luther's Works* (1534, Sermon series on 1 Corinthians 15), edited by Jaroslav Pelikan and Helmut T. Lehmann, American Edition, Vol. 28 (St. Louis: Concordia Publishing House; Philadelphia: Fortress Press, 1955–1986), p. 97.

[2]*Luther's Works*, Vol. 28, p. 99.

[3]*Luther's Works*, Vol. 28, p. 101. (Note: The American Edition translation of the phrase reads, in error, "a mere dream with sequel." The German reads, *ein lauterer Traum, da nichts nach folgt,* "a mere dream after which nothing follows." Consultation with the Concordia Historical Institute, St. Louis, Missouri.)

[4]*Luther's Works*, Vol. 28, p. 94.

[5]*Lutheran Worship* (St. Louis: Concordia Publishing House, 1982), pp. 141,142.

[6]Martin Luther, *Sermons of Martin Luther: The House Postils* (1532, Easter Eve, on the Second Article of the Apostles' Creed), edited by Eugene F. A. Klug, translated by Eugene F. A. Klug, et al., Vol. 1 (Grand Rapids: Baker Books, 1996), p. 476.

[7]Martin Luther, *Sermons of Martin Luther: The Church Postils* (1538, Easter Sunday, on Mark 16:1-8), edited by John Nicholas Lenker, Vol. 2 (Minneapolis: Luther Press, 1906), p. 249.

[8]Luther, *The Church Postils*, Vol. 2, p. 216.

[9]Luther, *The House Postils* (1534, First Sunday after Easter, on John 20:19-31), Vol. 2, p. 59.

[10]*Luther's Works* (1538, on the Three Symbols or Creeds of the Christian Faith), Vol. 34, pp. 210,211.

[11]*Luther's Works*, Vol. 28, p. 151.

[12]*Luther's Works*, Vol. 28, p. 148.

[13]*Luther's Works*, Vol. 28, p. 80.

[14]Luther, *The House Postils* (1535, Easter Monday, on Luke 24:13-35), Vol. 2, p. 31.

[15]*Luther's Works*, Vol. 28, p. 77.

[16]*Luther's Works*, Vol. 28, p. 66.

[17]Alister McGrath, *What Was God Doing on the Cross?* (Grand Rapids: Zondervan Publishing House, 1992).

[18]*Lutheran Worship,* hymn 123:2.

[19]Marc Lienhard, *Luther: Witness to Jesus Christ,* translated by Edwin H. Robertson (Minneapolis: Augsburg Publishing House, 1982), p. 54.

[20]Luther, *The House Postils* (1533, Easter sermon, on Mark 16:1-7), Vol. 2, p. 9.

[21]Luther, *The House Postils,* Vol. 2, p. 10.

[22]Martin Luther, *Galatians,* edited by Alister McGrath and J. I. Packer (Wheaton, Illinois: Crossway Books, 1998), p. 154.

[23]*Luther's Works* (1545, on Genesis 48), Vol. 8, p. 162.

[24]*Luther's Works* (1537, on John 14), Vol. 24, p. 137.

[25]*Luther's Works* (1515, on Romans 4), Vol. 25, p. 284.

[26]*Luther's Works* (1537, on John 16), Vol. 24, p. 346.

[27]*Luther's Works* (1532, on 1 Thessalonians 4), Vol. 51, p. 237.

[28]Luther, *Galatians,* p. 136.

[29]*Luther's Works,* Vol. 51, p. 241.

[30]Luther, *Galatians,* p. 29.

[31]Luther, *The Church Postils,* Vol. 2, p. 217.

[32]Luther, *The Church Postils* (1540, Sunday after Easter, on John 20:19-31), Vol. 2, pp. 383,384.

[33]Luther, *The Church Postils,* Vol. 2, p. 412.

[34]Martin Luther, *Commentary on Peter and Jude,* translated by John Nicholas Lenker (Grand Rapids: Kregel Publications, 1990), p. 26.

[35]Luther, *The House Postils,* Vol. 2, p. 27.

[36]Luther, *The House Postils,* Vol. 2, p. 28.

[37]Luther, *The Church Postils* (1524, Easter Monday, on Luke 24:13-35), Vol. 2, p. 297.

[38]*Luther's Works,* Vol. 28, p. 115.

[39]*Luther's Works,* Vol. 28, p. 113.

[40]*Luther's Works,* Vol. 28, p. 113.

[41]*Luther's Works* (1520, Fourteen Consolations), Vol. 42, p. 151.

[42]Luther, *The House Postils,* Vol. 2, p. 25.

[43]Luther, *The House Postils,* Vol. 2, p. 26.

[44]*Luther's Works* (1536, on Genesis 3:15), Vol. 1, p. 196.

[45]*Luther's Works,* Vol. 28, p. 98.

[46]*Luther's Works* (on Genesis 4), Vol. 1, p. 330.

[47]*Luther's Works,* Vol. 1, p. 285.

[48]*Luther's Works* (1539, on Genesis 22), Vol. 4, p. 158.

[49]*Luther's Works,* Vol. 4, p. 113.

[50]*Luther's Works,* Vol. 4, p. 96.

[51]*Luther's Works,* Vol. 4, p. 120.

[52]*Luther's Works,* Vol. 4, pp. 119,120.

[53]*Luther's Works,* Vol. 4, p. 136.

[54]*Luther's Works,* Vol. 4, p. 119.

[55]*Luther's Works,* Vol. 4, p. 119.

[56]*Luther's Works,* Vol. 8, p. 191.

[57]*Luther's Works* (1525, on Jonah 4:3), Vol. 19, p. 31.

[58]*Luther's Works,* Vol. 51, p. 246.

[59]Luther, *The Church Postils,* Vol. 2, p. 241.

[60]Hal. H. Hopson, "He Is Mine" (Carol Stream, Illinois: Hope Publishing Company, 1999).

[61]Martin Luther, *Martin Luther's Basic Theological Writings* (1546, Prefaces to the New Testament), edited by Timothy F. Lull (Minneapolis: Fortress Press, 1989), p. 116.

[62]*Luther's Works*, Vol. 42, pp. 163,164.

[63]Lienhard, *Luther: Witness*, p. 41.

[64]Luther, *The Church Postils*, Vol. 2, p. 241.

[65]*Luther's Works*, Vol. 24, p. 139.

[66]*Luther's Works*, Vol. 24, p. 142.

[67]*Luther's Works* (1532, Lectures on the Psalms), Vol. 12, p. 231.

[68]*Luther's Works*, Vol. 51, p. 242.

[69]Luther, *Galatians*, p. 105.

[70]*Luther's Works*, Vol. 28, p. 109.

[71]*Luther's Works*, Vol. 51, p. 316.

[72]Luther, *The House Postils*, Vol. 2, p. 16.

[73]*Luther's Works* (1537–1540, on John 3:4), Vol. 22, p. 283.

[74]Martin Luther, *Three Treatises* (1520, The Babylonian Captivity of the Church), translated by Charles M. Jacobs, A. T. W. Steinhauser, and W. A. Lambert (Philadelphia: Fortress Press, 1970), p. 191.

[75]Luther, *Three Treatises*, p. 191.

[76]*Luther's Works*, Vol. 28, p. 132.

[77]*Luther's Works*, Vol. 51, p. 325.

[78]*Luther's Works*, Vol. 51, p. 323.

[79]Luther, *The House Postils*, Vol. 1, p. 489.

[80]*Luther's Works* (1535, on Genesis 1:26,27), Vol. 1, p. 68.

[81]*Lutheran Worship*, hymn 223:7.

[82]*Luther's Works*, Vol. 24, p. 42.

[83]Luther, *Three Treatises*, p. 192.

[84]The Small Catechism, *The Book of Concord: The Confessions of the Evangelical Lutheran Church*, translated and edited by Theodore G. Tappert (Philadelphia: Fortress Press, 1959), p. 349.

[85]*Luther's Works*, Vol. 51, p. 244.

[86]Luther, *Three Treatises*, p. 193.

[87]*Luther's Works*, Vol. 24, pp. 42,43.

[88]Luther, *The Church Postils*, Vol. 2, p. 304.

[89]*Luther's Works*, Vol. 24, p. 48.

[90]*Luther's Works*, Vol. 24, p. 194.

[91]*Luther's Works*, Vol. 24, p. 194.

[92]*Luther's Works*, Vol. 24, p. 198.

[93]*Luther's Works*, Vol. 24, p. 195.

[94]Luther, *The Church Postils*, Vol. 2, p. 357.

[95]Luther, *The Church Postils*, Vol. 2, p. 356.

[96]Luther, *The Church Postils*, Vol. 2, pp. 285,286.

[97]*Luther's Works*, Vol. 42, p. 141.

[98]Luther, *The Church Postils*, Vol. 2, p. 253.

[99]*Luther's Works*, Vol. 12, p. 234.

[100]Luther, *The Church Postils*, Vol. 2, p. 358.

[101]Luther, *The House Postils*, Vol. 2, p. 37.

[102]*Luther's Works* (on Galatians 2:19), Vol. 26, p. 158.

[103]Luther, *The Church Postils*, Vol. 2, p. 247.

[104]The Large Catechism, Tappert, p. 418.

[105]*Luther's Works,* Vol. 24, pp. 246,247.

[106]*Luther's Works,* Vol. 28, p. 205.

[107]*Luther's Works,* Vol. 28, p. 205.

[108]*Luther's Works* (1529, The Marburg Colloquy), Vol. 38, p. 44.

[109]*Lutheran Worship,* hymn 123:5.

[110]Luther, *The House Postils,* Vol. 2, p. 35.

[111]Luther, *The House Postils,* Vol. 2, p. 61.

[112]Luther, *The Church Postils,* Vol. 2, p. 361.

[113]Luther, *The Church Postils,* Vol. 2, p. 302.

[114]*Luther's Works,* Vol. 24, pp. 403,404.

[115]*Luther's Works,* Vol. 24, p. 404.

[116]*Luther's Works,* Vol. 28, p. 101.

[117]Luther, *The Church Postils,* Vol. 2, p. 289.

[118]Luther, *The Church Postils,* Vol. 2, p. 397.

[119]John Cloud, "A Kinder, Gentler Death," *Time* (September 18, 2000), p. 64.

[120]*Luther's Works,* Vol. 28, p. 116.

[121]*Luther's Works,* Vol. 1, p. 196.

[122]*Luther's Works,* Vol. 28, p. 133.

[123]*Luther's Works,* Vol. 28, p. 133.

[124]Lull, *Basic Theological Writings* (1519, "A Sermon on Preparing to Die"), p. 640.

[125]Lull, *Basic Theological Writings,* p. 640.

[126]*Luther's Works,* Vol. 4, p. 105.

[127]*Luther's Works,* Vol. 42, p. 129.

[128]*Luther's Works,* Vol. 42, p. 130.

[129]*Luther's Works,* Vol. 24, p. 404.

[130]Bengt R. Hoffman, *Luther and the Mystics* (Minneapolis: Augsburg Publishing House, 1976), p. 214.

[131]*Luther's Works,* Vol. 26, p. 369.

[132]Daniel Callahan, *The Troubled Dream of Life* (Washington, DC: Georgetown University Press, 2000), p. 14.

[133]Lull, *Basic Theological Writings,* pp. 640,641.

[134]Lull, *Basic Theological Writings,* p. 642.

[135]*Luther's Works,* Vol. 51, pp. 239,240.

[136]*Luther's Works,* Vol. 51, pp. 237,238.

[137]Lull, *Basic Theological Writings,* p. 638.

[138]*Luther's Works,* Vol. 24, p. 37.

[139]*Luther's Works,* Vol. 24, p. 42.

[140]Heinrich Bornkamm, *Luther's World of Thought* (1522, Invocavit sermon), translated by Martin H. Bertram (St. Louis: Concordia Publishing House, 1965), p. 299.

[141]Luther, *The Church Postils* (1532, Second sermon, third Sunday after Easter), Vol. 3, p. 92.

[142]Bornkamm, *Luther's World of Thought* (1530–1532, on John 6–8), p. 129.

[143]*Luther's Works,* Vol. 28, p. 70.

[144]*Luther's Works,* Vol. 8, p. 194.

[145]Lull, *Basic Theological Writings,* p. 654.

[146]*Luther's Works*, Vol. 51, p. 232.

[147]*Luther's Works*, Vol. 51, pp. 232,233.

[148]Martin Luther, *What Luther Says: An Anthology,* compiled by Ewald M. Plass, Vol. 1 (St. Louis: Concordia Publishing House, 1959), p. 368.

[149]Luther, *The House Postils,* Vol. 1, p. 488.

[150]*Luther's Works,* Vol. 24, p. 44.

[151]*Luther's Works,* Vol. 24, p. 45.

[152]*Luther's Works,* Vol. 28, p. 120.

[153]*Luther's Works,* Vol. 28, p. 112.

[154]*Luther's Works,* Vol. 28, p. 112.

[155]*Luther's Works,* Vol. 24, p. 136.

[156]*Luther's Works,* Vol. 28, p. 108.

[157]*Luther's Works,* Vol. 28, p. 108.

[158]Luther, *The Church Postils,* Vol. 2, p. 243.

[159]*Luther's Works,* Vol. 28, p. 207.

[160]*Luther's Works,* Vol. 8, p. 162.

[161]Luther, *The House Postils,* Vol. 2, p. 15.

[162]Luther, *The House Postils* (1533, Sixteenth Sunday after Trinity, on Luke 7:11-17), Vol. 3, p. 33.

[163]*Luther's Works,* Vol. 28, p. 212.

[164]*Luther's Works,* Vol. 28, p. 71.

[165]Ewald M. Plass, *This Is Luther* (St. Louis: Concordia Publishing House, 1984), p. 259.

[166]*Luther's Works* (1530, letter to Hans Luther), Vol. 49, p. 271.

[167]*Luther's Works,* Vol. 49, p. 270.

[168]*Luther's Works* (1532, letter to Margaret Luther), Vol. 50, p. 18.

[169]*Luther's Works,* Vol. 50, p. 20.

[170]Hoffman, *Luther and the Mystics,* p. 206.

[171]Plass, *This Is Luther*, p. 270.

[172]Preserved Smith, *The Life and Letters of Martin Luther* (1546, letter to Katherine Luther) (New York: Barnes and Noble, Inc., 1968), p. 418.

[173]Smith, *Life and Letters,* p. 421.

[174]Bornkamm, *Luther's World,* p. 303.

[175]Smith, *Life and Letters,* p. 423.

[176]*Luther's Works,* Vol. 50, p. 318.

[177]*Luther's Works,* Vol. 28, p. 179.

[178]*Luther's Works,* Vol. 28, p. 178.

[179]*Luther's Works,* Vol. 28, p. 175.

[180]*Luther's Works,* Vol. 28, p. 179.

[181]*Luther's Works,* Vol. 28, p. 188.

[182]*Luther's Works,* Vol. 28, p. 182.

[183]*Luther's Works,* Vol. 51, p. 246.

[184]*Luther's Works,* Vol. 51, p. 239.

[185]*Luther's Works,* Vol. 51, p. 236.

[186]*Luther's Works* (1527–1530, on Isaiah 57:3), Vol. 17, p. 269.

[187]Plass, *What Luther Says*, Vol. 1, p. 385.

[188]Luther, *The House Postils,* Vol. 3, p. 73.

[189]*Luther's Works* (1538–1539, on Genesis 15:1), Vol. 3, p. 11.

[190]Plass, *What Luther Says,* Vol. 1, p. 385.

[191]*Luther's Works* (1522, on 1 Peter 3:19-22), Vol. 30, p. 114.

[192]Luther, *The Church Postils* (24th Sunday after Trinity, on Matthew 9:18-26), Vol. 5, p. 359.

[193]*Luther's Works,* Vol. 30, p. 114.

[194]*Luther's Works,* Vol. 30, p. 114.

[195]Paul Althaus, *The Theology of Martin Luther,* translated by Robert Schulz (Philadelphia: Fortress Press, 1966), p. 416.

[196]Plass, *What Luther Says,* Vol. 1, p. 387.

[197]Luther, *The House Postils*, Vol. 3, p. 32.

[198]Luther, *The House Postils,* Vol. 3, p. 34.

[199]Luther, *The House Postils,* Vol. 3, p. 34.

[200]Nancy Gibbs, "Baby, It's You! And You, And You," *Time* (February 11, 2001), p. 49.

[201]Gibbs, "Baby, It's You!" p. 49.

[202]*Luther's Works,* Vol. 28, p. 110.

[203]Luther, *The House Postils,* Vol. 1, p. 484.

[204]*Luther's Works,* Vol. 51, p. 252.

[205]*Luther's Works,* Vol. 51, p. 250.

[206]*Luther's Works,* Vol. 51, p. 250.

[207]Luther, *The House Postils,* Vol. 3, p. 31.

[208]*Luther's Works,* Vol. 28, p. 188.

[209]*Luther's Works,* Vol. 28, p. 142.

[210]*Luther's Works,* Vol. 28, p. 144.

[211]*Luther's Works,* Vol. 28, p. 171.

[212]*Luther's Works,* Vol. 28, p. 126.

[213]The Large Catechism, Tappert, p. 418.

[214]*Luther's Works,* Vol. 26, p. 274.

[215]*Luther's Works,* Vol. 28, p. 185.

[216]*Luther's Works,* Vol. 28, p. 187.

[217]*Luther's Works,* Vol. 28, p. 146.

[218]Cloud, "A Kinder, Gentler Death," p. 64.

[219]Callahan, *Troubled Dream,* p. 231.

[220]*Luther's Works,* Vol. 28, p. 72.

[221]*Luther's Works,* Vol. 28, p. 177.

[222]*Luther's Works,* Vol. 28, p. 178.

[223]*Luther's Works,* Vol. 28, p. 177.

[224]*Luther's Works,* Vol. 28, p. 117.

[225]*Luther's Works,* Vol. 28, p. 125.

[226]*Luther's Works,* Vol. 28, p. 98.

[227]*Luther's Works,* Vol. 8, p. 21.

[228]*Luther's Works,* Vol. 28, p. 98.

[229]*Luther's Works,* Vol. 28, p. 98.

[230]*Luther's Works,* Vol. 28, p. 72.

[231]*Luther's Works,* Vol. 8, p. 236.

[232]*Luther's Works,* Vol. 28, p. 71.
[233]*Luther's Works,* Vol. 28, pp. 73,74.
[234]*Luther's Works,* Vol. 8, p. 19.
[235]*Luther's Works,* Vol. 28, p. 202.
[236]*Luther's Works,* Vol. 51, p. 249.
[237]Luther, *The House Postils,* Vol. 2, p. 8.
[238]*Luther's Works,* Vol. 28, p. 99.
[239]Luther, *The House Postils,* Vol. 1, p. 483.
[240]*Luther's Works,* Vol. 51, p. 239.
[241]*Luther's Works,* Vol. 51, p. 235.
[242]*Luther's Works,* Vol. 28, p. 206.
[243]*Luther's Works,* Vol. 28, pp. 202,203.

 # Bibliography

Althaus, Paul. *The Theology of Martin Luther.* Translated by Robert C. Schulz. Philadelphia: Fortress Press, 1966.

Bornkamm, Heinrich. *Luther's World of Thought.* Translated by Martin H. Bertram. St. Louis: Concordia Publishing House, 1965.

Callahan, Daniel. *The Troubled Dream of Life.* Washington, DC: Georgetown University Press, 2000.

Cloud, John. "A Kinder, Gentler Death." *Time* (September 18, 2000), pp. 59-74.

Colum, Padriac. "Fates." *World Book Encyclopedia.* Vol. 7. Chicago: World Book-Childcraft International, Inc., 1979.

Gibbs, Nancy. "Baby, It's You! And You, And You." *Time* (February 11, 2001), pp. 46-57.

Hoffman, Bengt R. *Luther and the Mystics.* Minneapolis: Augsburg Publishing House, 1976.

Jonas, Justus, Michael Coelius, et al. *The Last Days of Luther.* Translated by Martin Ebon. Garden City, New York: Doubleday and Company, Inc., 1970.

Kolb, Robert. "God Kills to Make Alive: Romans 6 and Luther's Understanding of Justification (1535)." *Wisconsin Lutheran Quarterly,* Vol. 12, No. 1 (Spring 1998), pp. 33-56.

Kostlin, Julius. *The Theology of Luther.* Translated by Charles E. Hay. 2 vols. Philadelphia: Lutheran Publication Society, 1897.

Lienhard, Marc. *Luther: Witness to Jesus Christ.* Translated by Edwin H. Robertson. Minneapolis: Augsburg Publishing House, 1982.

Luther, Martin. *The Church Postils.* Edited by John Nicholas Lenker. 4 vols. Minneapolis: Luther Press, 1906.

———. *Commentary on Peter and Jude.* Translated by John Nicholas Lenker. Grand Rapids: Kregel Publications, 1990.

———. *Galatians.* Edited by Alister McGrath and J. I. Packer. Wheaton, Illinois: Crossway Books, 1998.

———. *Luther's Works.* Edited by Jaroslav Pelikan and Helmut T. Lehmann. American Edition. 55 vols. St. Louis: Concordia Publishing House; Philadelphia: Fortress Press, 1955–1986.

————. *Martin Luther's Basic Theological Writings.* Translated by Timothy F. Lull. Minneapolis: Fortress Press, 1989.

————. *Sermons of Martin Luther: The Church Postils.* Translated by John Nicholas Lenker, et al. Edited by John Nicholas Lenker. 8 vols. Grand Rapids: Baker Book House, 1983.

————. *Sermons of Martin Luther: The House Postils.* Translated by Eugene F. A. Klug, et al. Edited by Eugene F. A. Klug. 3 vols. Grand Rapids: Baker Books, 1996.

————. *Three Treatises.* Translated by Charles M. Jacobs, A. T. W. Steinhauser, and W. A. Lambert. Philadelphia: Fortress Press, 1970.

Lutheran Worship. St. Louis: Concordia Publishing House, 1982.

McGrath, Alister. *What Was God Doing on the Cross?* Grand Rapids: Zondervan Publishing House, 1992.

Plass, Ewald M. *This Is Luther.* St. Louis: Concordia Publishing House, 1984.

Plass, Ewald M., editor. *What Luther Says: An Anthology.* 3 vols. St. Louis: Concordia Publishing House, 1959.

Smith, Preserved. *The Life and Letters of Martin Luther.* New York: Barnes and Noble, Inc., 1968.

The Book of Concord: The Confessions of the Evangelical Lutheran Church. Translated and edited by Theodore G. Tappert. Philadelphia: Fortress Press, 1959.